WAITING
for ANSWERS

WAITING
for ANSWERS

A Parent's Guide
to Grief, Resolution,
and Healing

BETSY HAID

Deep River
BOOKS

Published by
Deep River Books
Sisters, Oregon
http://www.deepriverbooks.com

ISBN 10: 1-935265-42-3

ISBN 13: 978-1-935265-42-9

Library of Congress Control Number: 2011921107

Printed in the USA

Cover design by Robin Black, www.BlackbirdCreative.biz

TABLE OF CONTENTS

For Anna and Holly—all my joy and light.

Chapter One

INTO DARKNESS

"Like most misery, it started with apparent happiness."
—Marcus Zusak, *The Book Thief*

Spring comes early to Atlanta. By mid-April the whole city is cloaked in azaleas and dogwood blossoms, and the trees are budding in a brilliant green that glows like neon. The temperatures climb, and the sunsets stretch longer and longer into evening. Thousands of crickets and cicadas chirp at dusk. You can smell freshly cut grass everywhere you go, and the soccer fields and baseball fields are brimming with children.

On one of those idyllic April afternoons that seem so full of life, my five-year-old daughter, Virginia, was killed in an automobile accident. My whole world shifted on its axis that afternoon, and everything went spinning out of control. Everything I had ever believed about my future, my children's futures, my dreams, my values, my faith—everything—came flying apart.

People told me in the weeks following my daughter's death that I appeared to be holding up pretty well, that it looked like I was coping with the loss better than most mothers could have, and better than they would have expected. Sometimes these comments were spoken with kindness and concern. Sometimes they were meant as a criticism. On the surface I did appear to be functioning well. I was getting up every day and taking care of my surviving children; I was exercising and seeing friends; I was writing thank-you letters for all the flowers and meals we received after the accident. That appearance of normalcy was a thin veneer, though. Inside I was reeling. I was desperate to find answers and practical help. I needed to know how to keep from going mad and how to stay strong enough to take care of my two older daughters who had come oh-so-close to being killed that afternoon as well. I was gritting my teeth and getting through each day, but I knew I was slipping into darkness, and I was going to have to get help, serious help, if I was to make it through the grieving process.

If you are reading this book, chances are that you or someone you care about deeply has also lost a child, and you too are looking for guideposts, signs, or any type of map to help you navigate through this horrible experience. I hope that this book will act as such a map. I will tell you about my journey and all I learned along the way. I will tell you the things I did right, and I will tell you some of the unforgivable mistakes I made. I will tell you the stories of other people who have made it through the grieving process and come out to flourish on the other side. I will share with you the latest psychological research on loss and grief and give you all the information I can on how to take care of yourself and your family as you grieve and heal.

When I started writing this book, I didn't intend for it to be a "Christian book," but the more I read, the more I researched, and the more time and introspection I had, the more I realized that it was the power of my faith and the power of faith in the people around me, both Christian and Jewish, that allowed me to fully heal. You are dealing with the worst pain in the human experience, and you are going to need a guide with compassion and wisdom to help you make it through. You have that guide—that shepherd—in Christ, and you are never alone. You may doubt that guidance now, even reject the notion of it completely, but when your journey is over, you'll be certain that you had help beyond all human reckoning.

The afternoon of the accident, my daughters were riding home with their babysitter from a picnic at Stone Mountain Park, which is only a few miles from downtown Atlanta. The young woman, who had been our live-in babysitter for over a year, was finishing graduate school and getting ready to buy her first house. We knew she was leaving us soon, and the trip to Stone Mountain was a treat for my three girls before the amazing nanny whom they all adored moved on. Her brother, a teacher at a New England boarding school, was visiting his sister during spring break, and he went along on the picnic to help out with the girls. On the way home, all the children were buckled up in the backseat of the car, and our babysitter's brother offered to drive even though he wasn't familiar with Atlanta or the traffic. We'll never know exactly what happened on Highway 78 several car lengths ahead that distracted him and several other drivers. All we know is that our sitter's brother, driving in the left lane, had to slow the car down significantly. As he was trying to accelerate again, another driver going well over eighty-five miles an hour slammed into the back of our babysitter's Honda sedan, killing Virginia and injuring my other children.

I was at home by myself when I got the initial phone call. The information was horrible and so fragmented that I couldn't make sense of anything. There had been an accident, and the girls had been seriously injured. My older daughters were at one hospital; Virginia was at another. Our sitter and her brother were at a third hospital, both with concussions. Why? What had happened? How bad were these injuries, and why in heaven's name was everyone spread out in all these different hospitals? Why hadn't the ambulance taken them all to one place? How in the world could I get to everyone at once? The room started spinning in front of me. My instructions were to first get to the emergency room where Virginia had been taken, and then, as soon as possible, drive to Egleston Children's Hospital in Decatur where my older girls were being treated.

My husband, Daniel, was a general aviation pilot, and he had left earlier that afternoon with one of his law partners to fly to Texas on business. I had no way to reach him quickly, and I certainly didn't want to shock him with this sort of news about his children while he was flying. I started making phone calls, but I couldn't find anyone. My mother-in-law was out; my father-in-law and his wife weren't at home either. My minister was in a meeting, and my best friend was out of town. I needed to be two places at the same time and fast. It was maddening.

While I was dialing, desperate to find someone to help, another call came in from the nurses at Egleston Hospital urging me to hurry to the emergency room for my older daughters. I grabbed my cell phone and started driving. I was able to reach my next-door neighbor, and I told her what few details I had. This amazing woman did more good for my family and me in the next few hours than I would ever have thought it possible for one human to accomplish. She drove to Decatur to be with my twins while I rushed to see Virginia. She also started a "phone tree" with our neighbors and with mutual friends from our children's schools. The alarm went out, and God knows I needed the help.

The minute I got out of the car at the emergency room, I knew that Virginia had been killed. It was all over the faces of the nurses and physicians who met me at the door. I think I started screaming, but I can't say for sure. A nurse put her arm around me and told me that the doctor who was with Virginia would be finished soon, and afterward I could go into the examining room. I remember that the sun was beginning to set;

it was starting to get dark outside. As I recall this nearly ten years later, the room starts spinning again, and I feel sick to my stomach.

I remember a doctor telling me that, yes, Virginia had been killed. I remember someone whispering that they needed to finish cleaning Virginia up before I saw her. It was ice-cold in the ER as they led me into the examining room, and I had the sense that it was getting even darker outside. I remember the doctor telling me that Virginia had been killed instantly and that she had not suffered, and I prayed he was telling me the truth. I remember them all telling me to take as much time with her as I needed. I remember seeing my joyous little girl on a steel exam table dressed in a thin hospital gown. I remember sobbing, picking her up, and finding her, to my horror, already cold. I felt alone in the universe and totally disjointed from reality.

I don't know how long I stood there holding Virginia, but when I came back into the emergency room lobby, night had fallen. A chaplain met me, prayed with me, and told me he would help me begin to make funeral arrangements. I told him about my older daughters. I had to hurry. I had to think and start making what I hoped would be rational decisions. I had no choice but to take action, to make more phone calls. I didn't have time to fall apart. I had two surviving children who needed me immediately.

I picked a funeral home and signed the paperwork to have Virginia's body transferred. I left a message for my minister, and I contacted my sister-in-law and my mother-in-law's neighbor. I didn't want my mother-in-law to get this news while she was alone. She had lost a child of her own in an automobile accident years earlier; to have this happen again, this time to her grandchild, was beyond anything any human being should ever have to bear.

A good friend of our family, also a pilot, contacted the Federal Aviation Administration to get Daniel's plane on the ground as soon as possible. I was making decisions independently and with a bizarre sense of certainty and confidence. The whole situation was surreal. "This is not happening," I kept telling myself. "I'm going to wake up in my den on the sofa, and the kids are going to be walking in the door from the park. This is a nightmare, and I'm going to wake up any minute." I was in shock. Shock is a form of triage for the brain, I'm convinced, and it allowed me to keep functioning. In less than an hour, another one of my incredibly strong and resourceful friends showed up at the emergency room and drove me to the children's hospital in Decatur. I talked nonstop on that long drive, but I cannot recall one specific word I said. All I remember communicating to my friend was that once my husband found out what had happened, he would be hysterical with grief.

Once I got to Egleston, another wave of shock hit me. One of my twin daughters had a broken femur, and her sister had a cracked vertebra in her back, but thankfully her spinal cord was still intact. These weren't life-threatening injuries, but they were serious, and both of the children were in significant pain. My daughter's broken leg was going to need surgery. I listened with perfect calmness and attention while the orthopedic resident described several different surgical and casting techniques they could use for my daughter's femur.

I made what I thought was a sound choice, and then I looked up at that young physician and shook my head. "Tomorrow," I said, "I probably won't remember one word of what we've talked about here in the last few minutes." He nodded in agreement. The physicians and nurses at Egleston did such a good job caring for my children, and they also did their best to shelter me from the press and even from too many earnest friends arriving at once. Virginia's accident, a multi-car pileup with fatalities on Highway 78, was spectacular and gory enough to make the local television news that night.

When the girls were finally settled in a room, one of the nurses asked me if I wanted to go up to the hospital chapel. The pain medication had nauseated one of my daughters, but the nurse assured me she would stay beside her in case she threw up again. I thanked the nurse, but I knew I couldn't leave. "I have to be about the care of the living," I said. It sounded unnatural and contrived—not like anything I would have ordinarily said. It didn't even sound like my own voice. But that declaration set the tone for the rest of my grief.

Once Daniel landed his plane in Texas, I called him and told him everything that had happened. He was devastated, of course, and also terrified that perhaps all three of the girls had been killed or that I was understating how serious the twins' injuries were. Within a few hours he and his law partner were on a commercial flight back to Atlanta. I can only imagine what a brutal experience that flight must have been for him.

When Daniel arrived at Egleston in the early morning hours, I was already in the maelstrom. I had made the initial funeral arrangements without including him, but I simply hadn't had any choice. The same held true for my older daughter's surgical procedure. With grace, he never second-guessed or criticized those decisions. Within a few hours, I had met with our minister and had tried to comfort my in-laws. I had cleaned up blood and vomit from my surviving children, and I had hugged my best friends and prayed with them. I had also asked one of the nurses to gently remove one well-meaning but overwrought woman who had come to see the girls. I didn't just want her out of the girls' room; I wanted her off the hospital floor. I needed people who were there to work and fight with me, not folks given to histrionic wailing.

Physically and emotionally, I was feeling tough, confident, even arrogant. And then the initial shock started to wear off. Adrenaline is a powerful chemical: it's the juice that allows soldiers to keep going in combat; it's the stuff that allows surgeons to stay focused and alert when operations take ten, twelve, fourteen hours or even longer. I had gotten a jolt of adrenaline when I heard about the accident in the initial phone call without even realizing fully what had happened. While my adrenaline was flowing, I was able to do all the things I needed to do for my older daughters and for Virginia's funeral arrangements. When the adrenaline ran out, however, my confidence and bravado ran out as well. I was exhausted. The reality of what had happened to my daughter and my entire family began to seep in, and I began my long journey through the grief process.

Your first few hours in the grief process may have been completely different from mine, or you may see striking similarities. In the next two chapters we'll be looking at those similarities and differences: what makes the grief process universal in some respects, yet unique and completely individual in others. Later in the book, we'll be exploring healthy ways for you to cope and find help as you grieve, as well as pitfalls you'll want to avoid. I want you to endure this ordeal as well as humanly possible. I want you to arrive, finally, at a place of hope and affirmation, holding on to your faith and reclaiming the joy and energy of your life. More than anything else, I want you to be able to rebuild your life in such a way that it will serve as a positive legacy to the memory of your child. I want you to find peace.

If you are far along in the grieving process at all, you've probably already discovered to your horror that as bereaved parents, we are part of an enormous and ever-growing community of people who are dealing with this loss. You are not alone, but your sources of support as you heal will often come from the most unlikely individuals and places. Conversely, people you might expect to comfort you and work with you through your pain may be helpless or unwilling. Nothing will be as you expect. All the rules have changed. This is a frightening and sometimes lonely process, but there is no need for despair. You will never stop grieving your child, but with support and encouragement, you'll never stop healing, either. Come with me, and we'll go find those sources of healing.

Chapter Two

THE WORK OF GRIEF

"We must embrace our pain and burn it as fuel for our journey."
—Kenji Miyazawa

I've always hated the word *survivor*. For me, it summons up images of devastated refugees who struggle away from natural disasters or hollow shells of men who've escaped from prison camps. I wanted to be more than just a survivor of Virginia's death and my own grief. I felt I owed more to my older daughters and also to Virginia's memory. Virginia had been the most vibrant, joyous little girl imaginable. I owed her more than my living a life of despair.

But as much as I wanted to reengage in life, I also remember thinking daily, almost hourly at first, that I couldn't endure the pain of the loss. I couldn't go on feeling the way I did; I had to do something, anything, for relief—but I had no idea where to turn. I asked myself constantly in those first dark weeks where people found the energy to get up out of bed and stumble through the day after they'd lost a child. How did families rebuild and reconnect after the unthinkable had happened? How did individuals maintain or reclaim their faith in God once they had experienced this sort of tragedy? I was starving for information about which coping strategies worked for families and which ones didn't. I was often afraid I was losing my mind—losing my grip on reality. I had a daily yearning to turn back the clock and wake from the nightmare my family was experiencing.

Someone told me in the early hours after Virginia's death that all I really had to do was breathe. It was good advice, and truthfully, for the first few days after you lose your child, breathing is about all you're capable of doing. One breath after another, one foot in front of the other, and you'll make it through another day. And as those days pass, you'll feel some strength coming back, and you'll be ready to start the healing process. Hopefully you'll have some friends and family members around to support you.

Friends brought us casseroles and pots of soup, they brought flowers and cards, they loved us and supported us in the only ways they could. They also brought books—lots of books. In the first few weeks after Virginia's death, I received fifteen books about loss and the grieving process. Fifteen. I read every one of those books from cover to cover, and several of them I read twice. I anxiously combed those pages trying to uncover some formula that would provide answers and help me through the day. And I learned an important lesson, though not the one I was looking for: don't ever give a book about the grieving process to someone unless you've first read the book yourself. Most of what I read, while not worthless, was certainly weak. Some of the writing was religious pabulum, some was bleak and hopeless. A few of the books, such as Rabbi Harold Kushner's *Why Bad Things Happen to Good People,* I found sound and uplifting (even though I didn't agree with everything Rabbi Kushner wrote).

The key elements missing from most of the books for me were the day-to-day stories about how people managed to cope and survive after they'd lost a child. I wanted to know what to expect emotionally and what I could do to facilitate my healing and the healing of my daughters. For those insights, I had to rely on the experiences of the other men and women in my community who had lost their children and the help of the Reverend Ron Greer, a pastoral counselor in Atlanta, who had exceptional skill and experience working with bereaved parents.

Counselors and psychologists often talk about the "work" of therapy. If therapy for daily emotional struggle is "work," then the grief process after losing a child should be considered "hard labor." You're going to need to prepare yourself physically, emotionally, and spiritually for the task. Don't feel like doing any preparation? Feel like throwing this book at the wall? I understand that response, but thinking that way won't do you any good. The clock moves forward, your life moves forward, and the grief process sweeps you along whether you are ready or not. If you want to weather this ordeal as well as possible and stay functional for your surviving children, your spouse, and your profession, you've got to get ready.

How do you do that? Caring for yourself physically while you grieve is not an easy task, but it's the most concrete aspect of your work, and it may be the easiest to accomplish. A few nights after Virginia's death, our internist, a family friend, came by the house to see us. "I didn't bring you a casserole or a tray of sandwiches," she told us. "I've got something I think you're going to need more. I've got the names of several excellent counselors you can contact, I've got some simple instructions about how to take care of yourselves for the next several weeks, and as soon as you can manage it, I'd like to see you in my office for physicals."

Our internist had seen before what this level of grief could do to people physically as well as emotionally. She knew that our immune systems would be weakened and that our blood pressure would go up. When she and I talked later in her office, she told me that it was not uncommon for grieving people to get flu-like symptoms or mononucleosis. She instructed us to eat even if we had no appetite, and we were fortunate enough to have neighbors and friends from our church who provided meals to us for several weeks. She told us to lie down and rest even if sleep itself was impossible. She insisted that we stay hydrated and keep our alcohol consumption low. She urged us to get out of the house and walk or get some sort of exercise every day. Once again, we were lucky enough to have friends there to support us as we tried to do the things our internist suggested. So many of my friends walked with me in those first weeks after Virginia's death, and I'll never be able to fully convey how thankful I am for that incredible kindness. Walking with a grieving friend is one of the most compassionate (and courageous) things you can do, even if you walk in silence at first. You don't have to force any conversation. Conversation will ultimately come, and your presence and willingness to listen is more soothing and healing than any drug.

Taking care of yourself emotionally and spiritually is a bigger challenge. One of the best analogies I've heard about working through grief compares it to swimming in heavy surf. The waves pull you out before you're ready, and they force you under, choking you. Just when you think you'll drown or be crushed against the shore, the waves dump you back on the beach, where you gasp for air before the next surge pulls you under again. Coughing and sputtering, you keep swimming because you have no choice. Exhaustion and desperation are continual lead weights around your feet. One day, though, you realize that the waves of pain are farther and farther apart, and they aren't quite as strong. You know another wave is coming, but you realize you have the confidence and stamina to swim and make it back to shore. You are healing, and if you have supportive friends waiting for you on the beach, your time in the water is going to be much easier.

I wanted to get back to that safe, dry beach as quickly as I could. I wanted to reengage in my life and my surviving daughters' lives. I wanted to laugh and smile and feel genuine happiness again, but I wondered if I would ever get to that point. I also felt guilt—enormous, gargantuan, irrational guilt—not only about the circumstances of Virginia's death, but even about my need to feel normal again. To honor my daughter adequately, didn't I need to suffer deeply and perpetually? Did I deserve to do more than just hobble through the day and survive? Yes. And you do, too. I want you to come through the other side of grief strong, sustaining others, and living a full and gratifying life. Right now, simply brushing your teeth or driving to work under the pressure of your grief probably feels like a herculean task, and my suggestion of a "full and gratifying life" may make you furious (or you may not even have the emotional energy at this point to feel anything but numb). Yet even now, in the earliest hours of grief, you are starting to heal. How well and how completely you will heal is the issue.

The healing process after losing a child is like learning to walk again on a broken ankle. You may always walk with some pain and a limp, but if you set the break correctly, you won't be crippled.

For me, good counseling and prayer were the best ways to set the break. The decision to seek counseling after your child's death is deeply personal, but I cannot imagine going through the grief process without professional psychological help. The type of counselor you choose and the relationship you build with that individual will play a huge role in your healing, and I'll address how to find an effective and affordable counselor in chapter 5.

Chapter Three

SNOWFLAKES, FINGERPRINTS, AND THE STAGES OF GRIEF

"Nobody ever told me that grief felt so much like fear."
—C.S. Lewis

The stages of grief are well documented. Understanding those phases and knowing the time it takes for most people to move through them helped me stay grounded even while I was suffering. If you know what's coming emotionally, you can try to brace yourself, holding on to the knowledge that the pain you're experiencing won't last forever. Dozens of researchers have explored the grief process, and I don't want to overwhelm you with list after list of scientific studies, but I do want to give you an overview of some of the most well-respected work in the field and what it has shown so that you too can be prepared for what's going to hit you.

One thing you'll want to be aware of as you read this research is that the stages of grief are extremely *fluid*. That means people often move back and forth between the different stages of grief, and the levels often overlap. If you think you've moved through a phase of grief (anger, for instance), but weeks later you're feeling those same emotions again, don't be discouraged or think you are regressing. The shifting and overlapping of emotions as you move forward is a normal part of the process.

As early as 1969, Swiss psychiatrist and researcher Elizabeth Kubler-Ross described the five typical stages of grief in a landmark book entitled *On Death and Dying*.[1] Two other major pieces of research, the 1976 Tampa Bereavement Study and, most recently, the three-year-long 2006 Yale Bereavement Study, both seem to confirm most of Dr. Kubler-Ross's original findings. The terminology used to describe the different stages of grief has changed somewhat over time, and as mentioned before, the stages of grief seem to overlap more than originally thought, but overall the findings are consistent.

Kubler-Ross described the first stage of grief as *denial*, where grieving individuals simply cannot believe they've lost a loved one or that death is imminent. They aren't able to accept that this tragedy has happened to them. The next phase of grief, according to Kubler-Ross, is *anger*. In this phase bereaved parents or others accept that the loss is real, but they feel a sense of rage at the unfairness of the death. Following anger is the stage of grief known as *bargaining*, when parents try to strike a deal emotionally with nature, the universe, or God. Even though they realize intellectually that nothing can bring their child back to life, parents in this phase are often praying for God to turn back the clock or to take their lives instead of the child's; or they may promise to make significant changes in their lives if God will restore the child.

After a time, bargaining gives way to *depression*. In this stage of grief, people fully realize the inevitability of the loss and their inability to change it. Feelings of guilt and helplessness mark this phase, and many people will withdraw from friends and family in order to find the emotional and psychological energy to process the finality of losing a son or daughter. At last, bereaved parents will enter the final stage of grief, *acceptance*, where they reengage in work and relationships and begin to plan for the future, acknowledging that their child will not be a part of that future except in their memories.[2]

Most of Dr. Kubler-Ross's information came from her experiences in counseling patients who were dying from cancer or who had close family members who were terminally ill. The Tampa study and the Yale study used more traditional research methods with more formal clinical controls, but even with fundamentally different research methods, the findings from both projects supported in large part what Dr. Kubler-Ross had observed anecdotally nearly forty years earlier.

I especially like the Tampa and Yale studies because of the way the findings are presented. They're clear, the data make sense, and we can even graph stages and time frames to help us mark certain thresholds as we move through the grieving process. And seeing the differences in what the Tampa and Yale researchers described as opposed to Kubler-Ross provided me with affirmation of what I was experiencing. Several times as I was reading the findings from the Yale study, I said to myself, "Yes! That's exactly how I felt. They nailed it!"

Below, I've drawn from the 1976 Tampa study[3] to show the typical feelings and behaviors people report as they move through the different phases. The outline is helpful, but don't look on the descriptions and boundaries as being ironclad. While the stages of grief are valid, an individual's reaction in the different phases and the time in which he or she moves from one phase to another are as unique as that person's fingerprint or a snowflake. Truly, no two are the same.

- **Denial:** Often marked by physical symptoms of shock and disbelief, this phase is what you will experience immediately after you learn of your child's death or terminal diagnosis. The physical symptoms of shock can last for weeks or even months.

- **Awareness of Loss:** Guilt, rage, and oversensitivity are the hall-mark emotions here, and they move in tandem with the stages or anger and bargaining from the Kubler-Ross research. The Tampa study doesn't give a concrete time frame for when these feelings will be strongest, but in the later Yale study, you'll see that your feelings of anger will probably be most intense at around five months.

- **Conservation and Withdrawal:** Here, you'll usually experi-ence fatigue, withdrawal, and even physical illness. Feelings of despair are not uncommon at this point. These are the emotions we all associate with depression, and the Tampa study suggests that bereaved parents can carry these emotions intensely for up to three years. The possibility of living through a three-year stint of depression was not what I wanted to read while I was grieving, but unfortunately I found it to be true in my experience and the experience of many friends who had lost children.

- **Healing:** Acceptance takes root, and bereaved parents begin to take control of their lives again at this stage, forgiving others and themselves as they try to forge a new identity without their child. Usually these changes are well underway by eighteen months into the grieving process.

- **Renewal:** Bereaved parents at this point have developed a new self-awareness and have reengaged in work, family, and commu-nity. Many are reaching out to help others. Renewal depends on the successful resolution of the earlier phases of grief and sustained support and healing for the bereaved individual.[4]

In the Yale study, researchers took the information from the earlier work and refined it even further. For instance, *disbelief,* not full-blown denial, seems to mark the initial phase of loss, and while the difference in description might seem minor, for therapists trying to counsel bereaved families, the change is significant. These feelings of shock and disbelief began to fade at around four months after the child's death. *Yearning* was the overriding emotion that people in the Yale study described in the phase of grief previously known as *bargaining,* and this yearning seemed to occur earlier in the grief process than originally thought. (Yearning is truly what I felt after Virginia's death. I wasn't trying to strike a deal with God to bring her back, and I had a tight enough grasp on reality even in the first hours after the accident to acknowledge that the death had actually occurred, but the yearning I had for my child was overwhelming.)

The 2006 research confirmed that *anger* peaks in grieving parents at about five months and showed that as these feelings of anger peak and begin to diminish, the feelings of *depression* become even more intense. But after the six-month mark, the depression usually begins to subside as well.[4] This research confirms that the first six months after a child's death are going to be incredibly painful—the worst—but results from the Yale study are hopeful too. Even in the first few weeks of grief, feelings of renewal and acceptance were already showing up in the people they interviewed.[5] The healing starts early; you are going to feel better—and soon. A word of caution is necessary here, however. The feelings of healing and relief are going to be very short "breaks in the clouds" at first. You'll need to temper your hope with realism and acknowledge that the dark hours are going to far outnumber the good ones for a significant amount of time. Researchers can call the phases what they like and label the emotions as they please, but the studies prove again and again what we know intuitively: this is the work of grief that we cannot avoid or postpone.

The stages of grief apply to all of us, but reactions within the stages of grief are unique to each individual. In the initial shock after Virginia's death, Daniel's and my reactions couldn't have been more dissimilar.

Dan had difficulty eating anything, and he cried constantly. He cried so hard and for such long periods of time that he couldn't sleep or even rest. I cried, but not as much. The experience I had was constant vertigo: the room was always spinning, and I felt like I needed to hold on to chairs or tables for balance. I often felt that the floor was giving way beneath my feet, and of course, the symbolism of that response is sad and obvious. Even now, years after Virginia's death, when I think about the circumstances of the accident, I feel that same dizziness and the room starts to reel again. Many people in the early days of grief talk about feeling as though a tight metal band is wrapped around their chest, constricting their heart. No wonder *heartache* is such a powerful and accurate term for what you're feeling.

While some people can't sleep at all in the first few weeks of grief, I couldn't get enough sleep. It became a means of escape for me, and I could have easily slept twelve or fifteen hours a day. I also felt weak all the time even though I was eating well. I started to be frightened by the grief reactions of people around me. I had always considered Daniel to be the stronger of the two of us emotionally, yet he seemed to be struggling more with day-to-day activities and with our other children. On the surface at least, I seemed to be coping better with routine activities. Looking back on that time, though, I wonder if his initial response might not have been healthier and more authentic than mine. I was gritting my teeth, resisting grief, and trying to function at some false level of normalcy during the day, while he didn't try to tamp down or deny the enormity of the pain he was feeling.

Grief was draining the life out of us, and unfortunately, my immediate family could only offer limited help. My mother had died a year before Virginia's accident, and my father was a virtual invalid. I had no siblings. Ironically and tragically, my in-laws had lost a child of their own in an automobile accident twenty years earlier. As with so many bereaved couples during that time, they had no access to counseling or support groups, and I think much of their own grief must have gone unresolved. Their marriage ended in a painful divorce. I know my in-laws grieved deeply for Virginia and cared deeply for our family, but they simply could not give us the guidance we needed. These good people were still mired in their own loss and pain. Our help came from outside—from our church, from our friends, from our neighbors.

I could have never made it through those first few months without their concern, genuine love, and practical help. I am forever indebted to those remarkable people who brought meals to my table, walked with me, prayed with me, did my laundry, and helped me take care of my other children. I have never felt as much pain in my life as I did in the first few months after we lost Virginia, but neither at any other time in my life have I felt so much love and support from our friends. Seeing that outpouring of sympathy and concern gave me the courage to go forward on days when otherwise I couldn't have gotten out of bed.

Unlike many men, Daniel had a number of close friends. They embraced him literally and spiritually as soon as he got to the hospital the morning after the accident. They sat with him for two full days in the chapel of Egleston Hospital, giving him the time, space, and permission to grieve and cry openly. Those men, most of whom were from our church, still stand by him today, and in their expression of sympathy and support they demonstrated incredible compassion and Christian love.

In every phase of grief, Dan and I continued to respond differently to our pain. Anger infused all my grief. Everything even well-intentioned people said about the accident infuriated me. Daniel had much more grace on that front; he was able to see the kindness that was meant in a remark of sympathy even if the remark was brutally delivered. I fought depression tooth and nail with medication, counseling, and mile after mile of distance running (since Virginia's death, I've run four marathons and over twenty-five half marathons). At first Daniel was strongly opposed to my taking antidepressants, to counseling, and even to my rigorous physical exercise. He felt, perhaps legitimately, that my actions were keeping me from fully experiencing the pain of grief and that, consequently, I wouldn't fully heal. I saw his lack of action as keeping him stuck in depression. I read the fifteen books that our friends brought us; I don't think he read a single line. People grieve very differently.

One of the most interesting responses I saw from people (and we'll explore these responses more thoroughly later in the book) was a strong expectation about how grief was supposed to look in men as opposed to women. Many of these genuinely concerned people seemed disturbed and confused when our expressions of grief and behavior didn't meet their expectations. As early as the visitation the evening before Virginia's burial, people came up to Daniel at the funeral home and asked him to get his crying under control. They said he was upsetting people. Can you imagine such a cruel request? Of course you can—for you too are hearing unbelievable things come out of people's mouths about your own loss. On the other side of the spectrum, several people, notably older women at my church, told me that I needed to let go in public, to grieve and cry openly. None of these women had ever lost children of their own.

I remember reading that Jacqueline Kennedy was widely criticized after JFK's assassination because she was perceived as being too stoic and calm. People seemed disappointed that she didn't break down and cry openly in public; she didn't give them the show and drama they craved. Yoko Ono was vilified because she returned to work the day after John Lennon's funeral; she was painted as cold and heartless. I remember feeling outraged and sad on both women's behalf when I read these stories. How could anyone say that they weren't "grieving correctly" in public?

The individuals I came to know who had lost children didn't assign those gender grief expectations. They were wise and experienced enough to know that grief is a fingerprint. Your reaction is yours alone. Do not let others impose their notions about how and when you should grieve on you. Whatever you feel, do, or say in the next few months (with the exception of harming others or yourself!) is okay. You may not feel you have the right to say or do certain things, but put those thoughts aside. Seize the right. Grieve in your own way and on your own terms. No one should tell you how to feel or when to cry. There is no upside to losing a child; there is no silver lining. There is only consolation, and the most meaningful consolations I received after losing my daughter were the friendships I forged with people who had lost their own children or siblings. Their support, their empathy, and even their gallows humor kept me going day after day.

Chapter Four

HIKERS ON THE TRAIL

"The dogmas of the quiet past are inadequate in the stormy present.
This occasion is piled high with difficulty, and we must rise with
the occasion. As our case is new, so we must think anew and act anew."

—Abraham Lincoln

arly studies investigating the divorce rates for bereaved couples yielded pretty grim statistics. The divorce rates reported by research-ers in the 1980s often went as high as eighty to ninety percent.[6] Later studies, however, were much more hopeful. Two surveys of griev-ing families conducted by Compassionate Friends found that fewer than twenty percent of the couples who had lost children ended up filing for divorce within three years.[7] That's a huge discrepancy in study results to say the least; all it really tells us is that more research is needed to get an accurate picture of how the loss of a child really impacts marriages and divorce rates.

No matter where the research leads us, blanket statistics don't offer much practical help or solace when you're trying to hold *your* marriage together under the intense stress of grief. You'll want to look at your partnership, your family, and your overall circumstances, and you'll want to do all you can to sustain your marriage. As my grief counselor, the Reverend Ron Greer, said, "For couples who lose children, the experience is going to have a profound impact on the marriage, either good or bad. Strive to make it good."

The goal of this chapter is to look at the factors that dissolve marriages while couples are grieving and also to explore ways of working through the grief together as a team instead of letting the pain pull you apart.

My marriage of twenty years ended in divorce. Virginia's death, and more importantly, the situations that arose as Dan and I grieved so differently were the catalyst for the final breakdown. However, as Ron Greer reminded me, grieving differently is not always a marital negative. If I'm totally candid, I suspect my marriage would have eventually ended in divorce even if Virginia had not died. Her death, however, accelerated the dissolution and made it even more painful. People ask me what went wrong—how things unraveled—and I asked that same question of other couples who had gone their separate ways after losing their child. I also posed the question to the people I knew who had managed to save their marriages. How did they do it? Most of the current research suggests that the circumstances of the child's death, whether suddenly by accident, crime, or combat, or over time by illness or disease, doesn't seem to affect divorce rates.[8] So what does?

One of my dearest friends, Debbie Schecter, lost her son to cancer five years before Virginia died. Her insights and compassion, five years out in front of my own grief, played a huge role in my healing. This kind and capable woman is now a therapist and counselor in the Washington DC area. While Debbie and her husband eventually divorced, they were able to hold their marriage together for nearly twenty years after they lost their little boy. Debbie's description of what happens to marriages after the death of a child was elegant. As we were walking one day, she said, "Your marriage before you lose your child is like a porcelain teacup. It's beautiful, but fragile too. Once you lose your child, it's as though someone takes that teacup and dips it in india ink. All of sudden all those flaws and cracks are visible. They're ugly, and there's no denying them anymore."

Debbie's marriage survived as long as it did after her son's death because, according to Debbie, she and her husband had very realistic expectations of each other as they grieved. They began their actual grief process months before their son's death when they learned he would not survive his cancer. Debbie and her husband had been professional colleagues as well as husband and wife throughout their relationship, and they also had a tremendous sense of commitment to their older son. They left town shortly after their son's funeral, taking the first real vacation they'd had since their son's illness was diagnosed. Caribbean vacation? Right after your child's death? You bet. For them, it worked. Never pass judgment on what families and couples do to try to hold things together after they lose a child. For this couple, the vacation was an escape from the sterile halls of the hospitals and the awful stillness of their home without their little boy. Debbie and her husband could hold each other, cry, but be away from the physical reminders of the disease that had claimed their son.

I interviewed another couple, Kim and Roger, who were able to hold their marriage together after their young son was killed in an automobile accident. They discovered as they moved through the first year of their loss that they were intuitively alternating their episodes of intense grief. On one day, Kim would cry and grieve openly while Roger ministered to her and held her. A day or two later they would change places. If you use this method, you and your spouse will have the time and space you need to scream, cry, and even rage at God, knowing that your spouse is beside you, loving you and supporting you through your pain. This sacrifice and support can initiate tremendous healing. Likewise, forcing yourself to put your own pain aside for a little while to care for someone you love can give you a sense of purpose and focus even on your worst days.

For every couple whose marriage survives, there is another couple that doesn't make it. Why? Guilt and blame are two destructive emotions that claim many marriages, but they are inescapable feelings in the grieving and healing process. Charlotte, a woman in my old neighborhood, lost her son in a drowning accident during a community cookout and swimming party. Even though her husband was also at the party, he blamed Charlotte for not being vigilant enough, for not being a good enough mother. Not surprisingly, they divorced. Conversely, a close friend from my hometown also lost her little boy in a drowning accident, but her husband supported her, listened to her, and assuaged her guilt. This couple is still together, and they had little if any professional counseling. None was available in the small town where they lived.

In many cases couples undergo terrible financial stress if their child's death is caused by a prolonged or chronic illness. Even the hospitalization and burial costs after losing a child to an accident or suicide can be catastrophic. To suffer the death of your child and then not have the resources to get counseling, even if it is available, adds another layer of hardship. Many people don't have the money to order a pizza while they're grieving, much less pay for therapy or take a vacation. Money problems, as everybody knows, can cause strife in any marriage, and those problems are even uglier and more visible cracks in the teacup for bereaved families. (In the next chapter we'll explore ways to find effective counseling even if your financial situation is shaky.)

With the clarity of hindsight, I can see the issues and even the specific moments and words that caused my marriage to disintegrate. I call them "love killers." Daniel and I not only reacted to our grief in vastly different ways, but we moved through the stages of grief at different rates. As I mentioned before, I was angry with everyone and everything for months while Dan, relatively free of anger, seemed mired in depression instead.

When I tried to explain to a friend what had happened in the breakup of my marriage, I described the slow buildup of resentment and irresolvable hurt in this way:

Suppose you and your spouse are hiking side by side along a steep trail. You both take terrible falls when your child dies. You both suffer broken ankles, but the bones are broken in different places, causing excruciating but different pain reactions in both of you. You struggle to reach your spouse, but your hurt and *the distance you are from each other before the fall* makes it impossible for you to offer much encouragement or any type of practical help. You are both crying in agony, but even if you could reach each other, the severity of your injuries makes supporting each other for more than a few steps difficult.

To make matters worse, even though your pain is real, those bulky hiking boots hide the extent of your break, and you begin to wonder how badly hurt your partner really is. Is he crying out too much and complaining too much when actually, your pain is worse? He wonders the same thing about you. Yet you struggle along, because if one of you stops on that trail, night and cold will come along, and you won't survive the exposure. You find a way to limp along, to make some progress, but your mate cannot do the same, and he or she seems angry and resentful that you've been able to find a way to move forward—to heal. Your spouse seems to believe that her grief and pain are somehow more significant or important that yours because she can't go further when you can. Your individual pain often becomes more precious and exquisite to you than your relationship. Your resentment grows, and you have to authentically admit those feelings to each other. That honesty and brutal admission on an unforgiving trail are sometimes too much for the marriage to bear.

You have already suffered such an incredible loss in the death of your child. You shouldn't have to face even more agony with the pain of a divorce, and neither should your surviving children. Work with your counselor on keeping your marriage healthy from the start, and be forthright with your spouse if you feel hurt or resentful—but do the best you can to temper all you say with compassion. Employ the method that Kim and Roger used in alternating periods of open grieving and caregiving; share the burden of grief with your spouse, but don't forget to minister to him or her as well. The first several years after you lose your child are going to test you and your marriage brutally on nearly every level, but with faith, good counsel, and genuine concern for your spouse, you both can weather that test and gain a stronger marriage than you ever thought possible.

Chapter Five

ABLE COUNSEL

*"All the sorrows can be borne if you put them
into a story or tell a story about them."*

—Isak Dinesen

If you make the decision to go for counseling after your child's death, and I highly recommend that you do, the next challenge is finding a therapist who is affordable and will genuinely help you. The first counselor Dan and I saw was a kind and gentle man who didn't help us one bit. After several sessions, we were going over the same ground time after time without making any progress that I could see. It was expensive, it was time-consuming, and the sessions only seemed to make things more painful for my husband. We quit. The counselor wasn't a bad person or a poor clinician; he simply didn't have the specific training and expertise we needed.

At that point Daniel didn't want to go forward with any more therapy, but I knew I was going to have to have more help or I'd have difficulty staying functional and being able to care for my older daughters.

On the recommendation of a friend, I contacted a Methodist minister and pastoral counselor by the name of Ron Greer. Ron and his wife had lost their child in an automobile accident too, and Ron obviously had interest and insight into grief counseling.

Over the next two years, Ron Greer and I explored dozens of aspects of the grief process and how they were affecting my psychological and spiritual state as well as how those situations impacted my marriage and children. His counsel and the practical strategies he offered for working through my grief and helping my other children were invaluable. I still count my relationship with Ron and his wife (who ironically ended up teaching both of my daughters later in middle school) as one of the greatest blessings of my life. And while Ron is not the pastor of my church, I will always consider him one of the finest ministers I have ever known.

As you look for a counselor (and I hope you'll be lucky enough to find a Ron Greer in your community), you'll need to look at three factors: accessibility, affordability, and fit.

If you live in an urban area of any size, you should be able to find a list of therapists without any trouble. Beyond the Yellow Pages (which I do not recommend as a good referral source!), you should be able to get good recommendations from your family doctor, from your friends, or through your church or synagogue. Often, hospital social workers will also have useful resource lists. The Compassionate Friends website has links to qualified therapists nationally, as does the American Association of Pastoral Counselors (we'll talk a bit more about Compassionate Friends later in this chapter). If you're in a small town or rural area, things become more problematic. I strongly suggest that you take the time to find a good counselor, even if he or she is not within a convenient driving distance. Have the first few therapy sessions face-to-face, and then if the counselor is open to the option, alternate phone calls with actual visits. Even if you can only counsel for a few months, I believe it will pay off.

What about the cost? Therapy is expensive, and even though it's money well spent, the costs of a full therapeutic program are beyond the means of many families even if they have decent health insurance coverage. Luckily, many churches and charitable organizations are able to offer excellent counseling services on a sliding fee scale based on income. In some cases, therapy may even be free of charge.

You may also want to consider group therapy as opposed to individual counseling. The cost will almost certainly be less, and many people find group situations in which they can share common experiences and exchange ideas to be a good alternative to one-on-one counseling.

Another resource to investigate is Compassionate Friends. Initiated by two grieving families in Coventry, England, in 1967, this organization now has chapters all over the United States and Europe. Their support groups "offer bereaved families a chance for community and exchange in a welcoming environment at no cost." For more information about Compassionate Friends and to locate a chapter close to you, go to their website at www.compassionatefriends.org. Group therapy is not for everyone, especially in the early stages of grief. Go with your gut. Seek out the best therapeutic fit for yourself and your spouse, but be open to trying different approaches as your move through the different stages of bereavement.

The final consideration in finding a counselor is the most critical: fit. Mediocre counselors abound, and more often than not, otherwise competent therapists simply haven't had the training and experience to effectively help people with this level of grief. Ask. Or have a friend or family member do some homework for you. Do a little Internet research—Google your potential counselor. What personal experience does this therapist have in the grieving process? What is this counselor's primary area of interest or expertise? If you can find someone in your area with experience and training in dealing with bereaved families, put that person high on your prospect list. And obviously, you've got to trust, like, and connect with the person you're going to be working with. You'll know intuitively and prob-ably immediately if you and your counselor are going to have the type of rapport you need to work through your grief.

Many churches offer the services of a group of individuals known as Stephen Ministers. These volunteers are trained to serve as sources of emotional support for members of the church and for people in the broader community who are experiencing difficulty or transition in their lives. However, Stephen Ministers are not professionally trained or certi-fied counselors. You might find a Stephen Minister an excellent adjunct to your regular therapist, but I would strongly discourage you from using a Stephen Minister as your only source of counsel through the grief process. I think most Stephen Ministers who have completed their training would give you the same advice. A well-meaning but misguided Stephen Minister in my church offered to help me work through my grief after Virginia's death, and the things she said to me in that phone call broke every rule of sound counseling. I was furious and fighting back tears when I got off the phone with her, and had it not been for the calm advice of Ron Greer, I think I would have snapped. Unfortunately, my mother-in-law had a similar experience with a Stephen Minister in her own church. The Stephen Ministers organization offers a positive and helpful service, but keep in mind that they are trained volunteers, not professionals, and you should not expect professional-level counsel-ing services from them.

The good news is that more qualified, capable therapists and more affordable, effective programs are accessible now than ever before. The stigma of seeking counseling, especially in grief situations, has virtually disappeared. Let your friends and relatives help you seek out the best people and programs for your needs, and if you know anyone who has gone through the experience of losing a child, their recommendations for strong counselors should go to the top of your list.

Chapter Six

THE TOP TEN AWFUL THINGS PEOPLE SAY

*"Every evening I turn all my worries over to God.
He's going to be up all night anyway."*
—Mary Crowley

"Poetry is about the grief. Politics is about the grievance."
—Robert Frost

People mean well. Almost without exception, the things they say to you after your child's death are meant to express genuine sympathy and offer comfort. So much for good intentions! I wish I could take everyone at wakes, visitations, and funerals aside and tell them that all they have to say is, "I'm so sorry for your loss. I'm thinking about you all the time." All they have to do is give a hug or a pat on the back, because beyond those simple words and gestures, saying or doing anything for grieving parents in those early, raw hours is treading on thin ice.

43

When I think back over all these years to some of the things people said to my family and me after Virginia's death, I want to shake my head and laugh. At the time, though, laughter wasn't in the mix. If the stages of grief are inescapable, then so too must be the endurance of the awful things people feel they must say.

As I walked with Debbie Schecter for countless miles through my old neighborhood, she and I often talked about the differences and similarities of our faiths, our families, and the impact our grief had on our surviving children. But without fail, we talked about the outrageous comments people had made to both of us. She and her husband turned those scud bombs of sympathy into fabulous black humor. They began a list of the "Top Ten Awful Things" that people had to say, and as they had dinner together or sat in the evenings remembering their son, they'd share the best barbs of the day. Of all the atrocious comments made, something that Debbie's rabbi said still tops the universal most-awful list. He came up to her after a service at their synagogue and said, "So, Debbie, other than your son's death, how was your summer?"

No doubt you can start your own top-ten list, and while the first weeks or even months of your grief will find you too distraught to laugh about anything, later you'll find some humor and ironically even some solace in what people say. I remember feeling guilty the first time I laughed at a joke after Virginia died. My husband wouldn't be able to laugh for several more months, but I was hungry to laugh and find humor and normalcy in something, anything. When I did laugh for the first time, I couldn't stop. Like a kid trying to stifle the giggles in class, I was overcome with the hilarity of the simplest joke. Don't allow others to make you feel guilty when you want and need to laugh again: it's a sure sign of healing, and your child would want you to be able to laugh and find joy.

One of the worst comments I endured came from a long-time friend and neighbor of my parents. This man and his wife telephoned me shortly after Virginia's funeral to express their concern. This poor man, struggling to find some words of sympathy for me, said, "If you pray long enough, I'm sure you'll see what you did to anger God enough that he felt he had to do this to your family." I had to struggle not to slam the phone down on the cretin who would say such a cruel and idiotic thing. This same man, though, had taken wonderful care of my father after my mom passed away, and the voice of grace told me not to hang up. Boy, did I want to. Once again, people *mean well*. Also making my top-ten-awful list was the comment from the mom of one of Virginia's classmates: "God needed another rose for his garden, so he plucked Virginia." I wanted to pluck this woman's eyes out.

I have tremendous admiration and respect for the Reverend Chick Thorington, the retired minister of Northwest Presbyterian Church. He had a wise and pragmatic answer for questions that grieving people asked him about heaven, hell, and the afterlife and whether certain people were "saved" or not. He always replied that those questions would be answered in the full-ness of time, and all bereaved souls needed to know at that point was that God was always present, always loving them, and always loving and caring for the spirit of the person they had lost. Smart answer—correct answer.

In sharp contrast to Chick's sensitive and wise comments came the words in a eulogy from a school chaplain who spoke at the funeral of a sixteen-year-old boy from my daughters' school. This teenager had been killed in a car crash on a rainy evening as he went to return a couple of rented DVDs—a tragic and senseless loss of life and potential. The chaplain began his remarks by saying that he didn't know if this young man was in heaven or not, and he had serious doubts about the child's relationship with God. He addressed the parents and the classmates of this sixteen-year-old by adding that none of us really knows what another person's relationship is with God, and we can never say with certainty whether any person is reunited with Christ.

I went to the funeral with my close friend and running partner, and she literally had to restrain me as the chaplain spoke. I wanted to run down the aisle to the pulpit and slap this monster who had the audacity to call himself a minister (see, I told you I struggled with anger). As soon as I got home from the service and got my rage under control, I called the school's headmaster and requested that she fire the chaplain. I'll bet I wasn't the only parent to call with that request. I cannot imagine the pain those comments must have caused the boy's already devastated family. Theological issues such as the one the chaplain brought up are worthy questions for seminary classrooms and Bible-study small groups, but they shouldn't be touched at a funeral.

Understandably, a prime source of misdirected comments is parents who are terrified that what has happened to you today could happen to them tomorrow. That fear is well founded. We cannot live our lives in the shadow of fear, but there is no denying that an automobile accident or a terminal diagnosis could claim any of us or any of our children without warning. My older daughters took group ice-skating lessons, and as soon as they had recovered enough from their injuries to start skating again, I got them back out to the ice rink for their lessons. I wanted them to return to a normal routine (or whatever would pass for the "new normal" in our lives). I wanted them to see their buddies and exercise again; it seemed critical for their overall recovery and healing. The mother of another little girl in their class came up to me and said, "What in the world are you doing out of the house again so soon? Didn't you care about your younger daughter?" Simply typing her comment makes me grind my teeth.

You'll encounter another strange creature in the grieving process: the individual who gets tremendous gratification from offering comfort and words of sympathy. These same individuals often seem insulted if you don't want or need their particular brand of solace. May God give you grace and patience in your encounters with these people! My grace was often in short supply. Another woman came up to me at the ice rink a week or so later and said, "When are you going to fall apart so that I can help you put the pieces back together?" I barely knew this woman. I didn't have the mental energy to tell her that I fell apart sobbing every night when I got in the shower and that my husband and I broke down and cried every morning together as we poured our coffee. This woman's comments were ultimately thoughtless, selfish, or both. These types of people are more consumed with their own needs and their desire to feel good about themselves than they are interested in expressing genuine compassion. My hope is that you run into very few of these characters as you work your way through the grieving process!

While I heard some astounding, thoughtless comments, I was also lucky enough to have people in my life who said the most beautiful, comforting words, and I was blessed to talk with other grieving parents who had received similar support from their friends. Although I may sound harsh toward some people who were earnestly trying to do and say the right thing, the truth remains that we need people to talk to us even when what they say falls flat; we need people to tell us what they think and feel about our loss. We need to connect with others as we grieve. One of the few good things that comes out of losing a child is that you are able to talk with other bereaved parents, no matter what the stage of their grief, and usually offer some solace.

If you're reading this as a family member or friend of a grieving person, you're probably asking yourself, "Oh my gosh, what in the world can I say that will express my sorrow and offer support? How can I avoid saying something that will end up on someone's top-ten-awful list?" It's really not too hard. Don't try to explain God or God's will to a grieving parent. Don't compare the loss of your parent or your grandparent to the loss of a child. All these deaths are painful and difficult, but the loss of a child is in another category of agony. The death of a child, at least in our postmodern society, is out of the natural order of life. All you really need to do is tell the parents that you can't imagine the pain they're enduring and that you're truly sorry for them. We'll explore more ways to offer support in the next chapter and in chapter 18.

Chapter Seven

THE MOST COMPASSIONATE

"An individual should hold an awareness of God and His love at all times.
He should not separate his consciousness from the divine while
he journeys on the way, nor when he lies down, nor when he rises up."

—Nahmanides, Spanish rabbi (circa 1300 CE)

Some of the most compassionate people I encountered after Virginia's death were the mothers of the Jewish children in Ginny's preschool class. These women knew that Dan and I were practicing Christians, and they were wise and tactful enough to avoid giving us religious platitudes. I never heard "This is God's will" from any of them. Perhaps they were hesitant about treading on spiritual ground for fear of saying something hurtful or inappropriate to us; I don't know. All I know is that these women showed up day after day with food, practical help, gifts of artwork from their children, photos of Virginia playing with their children, plenty of hugs, and no judgment. I will always love and remember the women and children of the Day School's "Superstars" class for five-year-olds.

If you are reading this as a grieving parent, you know what I am getting ready to say. If you are reading this as a concerned friend or family member, read carefully: do not ever tell a grieving parent that his or her child was taken as a part of God's greater plan or as a punishment for some sin committed by the child or the parents. Who among us can begin to explain the will and workings of God in these circumstances? How incredibly arrogant would that be? Take a lesson from the wise women of the Day School. Even if you're lost a child yourself, keep your mouth shut about what you think God had to do with the loss of another person's son or daughter! The God I worship does not kill innocent children, and Christ expresses God's heart in the Gospel of Matthew when he tells the disciples, "Your Father in heaven is not willing that any of these little ones should be lost" (Matthew 18:14). The God I worship grieves with me in the loss of my child, and God grieves with you as well. He gets it; he's been there with his own Son; and his grief and loss stand as the greatest sacrifice in the history of mankind.

The God I worship will be with you in the deepest moments of your grief and despair, and God will give you the strength to heal and move forward. You are never alone, and our benevolent and all-loving God is sheltering and nurturing your child's spirit at this very moment. I have no doubt that we will see our children again. What form this will take and how it will happen is, I believe, beyond the scope of human intellect to comprehend, but I am convinced it will happen. As St. Paul said in his letter to the Thessalonians, "Brothers and sisters, we do not want you to be ignorant about those who fall asleep in death . . . do not grieve as the rest of men who have no hope" (1 Thessalonians 4:13). We may suffer terrible pain, but we are never without hope.

All of this leads us to the most difficult question in Christian theology. If God is all-loving, all-knowing, and all-powerful, why do innocent children suffer and die every day? Theologians, philosophers, and writers far more gifted than I have debated these questions for centuries, and the answers are always incomplete and frustrating. The fact is that no answer is going to satisfy a grieving parent, because all the explanations are wrapped in the limiting blanket of human language and human intellect. I don't think we have the capacity to even faintly comprehend why and how these things happen. It's like trying to explain calculus to a toddler.

Of course, I have my thoughts on the subject. I think that a partial answer is revealed in the Old Testament book of Job (we're going to spend some time with Job in a later chapter). I think part of the answer lies in how God structured the order of the universe and the laws of physics, and I think part of the explanation is tied up with the concept of free will and choice. There is a movement in current philosophy and psychology suggesting that we really don't have free will and choice, but I don't agree with that position, although I readily admit that there is much in the world we can't control. But there is much we can control—or at least influence. The man who killed my daughter chose to drive his car at over eighty-five miles an hour, and he chose to tailgate. His choices led directly to Virginia's death and the serious injury of four other people.

Where do we go with all these impossible questions and all this pain? Where do we find any comfort? I wish I had an easy answer for you. I wish I had any type of definitive answer. Even though I accept the fact that I will never understand the order of the universe or the will of God, that acknowledgment doesn't stop me, all these years later, from trying to untangle the mystery. Here's the best explanation I can give you, based strictly on my personal religious views and all my personal heresies:

God keeps time by a different wristwatch. In the scope of time-space and within the framework of eternity, the pain, separation, and overwhelming sense of loss we feel will not last long. This earthly life is over for all of us in the cosmic blink of an eye; you are going to be reunited with your child in a few sweeps of the second hand on that celestial clock. It hurts terribly now, but take heart. This pain will soon be gone. And never forget that Christ is with you as your source of comfort and reassurance while this earthly time drags on.

It would be easy for cynics and nonbelievers to cut my explanation to ribbons. That's all right. This is my answer for my grief. I don't know if it will bring you any comfort or insight, but I hope it will. More than anything, I want to offer you something that will bring you even a few moments of solace, relief, and most importantly, peace.

Do you think there are coffeehouses in heaven? I hope so. If there are, I want to sit down with Mary Magdalene and the apostle John, order a huge pot of decaf for the table, and ask them for the answers to all the complex and disturbing questions of our faith. I think they'd be particularly insightful on these issues. I'd invite you to join us: I'd invite everyone who had ever lost a child to join in the conversation—you sit by Abraham Lincoln; I'll sit by King David. We're going to need a big table. Come early so you can get a good seat, because our magnificent Creator is going to show up and settle all the debates. One day, one day.

Chapter Eight

MAGICAL THINKING

"The soul is indestructible, and its activity will continue throughout eternity. It is like the sun which to our eyes seems to set at night; but has in reality only gone to diffuse its light elsewhere."

—Goethe

I picked up a copy of Joan Didion's powerful memoir *A Year of Magical Thinking* on the recommendation of a friend, and I was startled by its tone and scope. I was also reminded again of how differently people respond to loss and uncertainty as they move through the grieving process. In the book, Didion explores the overwhelming grief she felt after her husband's sudden death and during the subsequent life-threatening illness of her daughter—a one-two punch of heartache. Her "magical thinking" focused on her wish to turn back the clock and return her husband to life as well as her yearning to provide her daughter with a full recovery from a devastating series of medical problems that confounded some of the best physicians in the country.

The psychological concept of magical thinking, which I discussed in my therapy sessions with Ron Greer, certainly addressed my longing to turn back the clock, but our discussions branched off and went in a totally different direction from Didion's experience. The information Ron Greer gave me about magical thinking and the strategies he suggested for dealing with it were some of the most helpful tools he gave me for practically working through my own issues and especially for helping me understand the grief and guilt of my surviving daughters.

In one of the first sessions I had with Ron, he asked me if my daughters blamed themselves for the accident or felt guilty about Virginia's death. I was astonished by the question.

"Well, of course not," I said. "They know they're innocent victims of an accident, and they played no role in what happened."

"Have you specifically asked them?"

"Well, no, but . . ."

"Ask them," Ron urged me. "I think you'll be surprised at what they have to say."

He went on to explain that children beginning at about five years of age commonly believe in magical thinking. For instance, a child may think that if he or she has ever wished that a certain classmate would fall off a bicycle, and if that classmate later did take a spill, then the child might earnestly believe that their negative thoughts actually caused the fall. It's easy to see that belief system carried out, even with adults, in different cultures around the world. It's the same sort of thinking that produces the concept of hexes, curses, or the evil eye.

I went home that afternoon after my session and asked the girls if they had any feelings of guilt or blame about the accident, and I was amazed when they said that they did. Ron had been right. Normal sibling rivalry being what it is, the twins told me that they had often been jealous of their baby sister, and they admitted that they sometimes had cruel thoughts about her or had "wished she wasn't around." I took plenty of time to let them tell me what they were feeling, and I tried to explain as best I could what had happened in the accident. I took several opportunities to reassure them that they were completely innocent. They had done nothing wrong, and I made sure they understood that the feelings of competition and jealousy they sometimes felt toward their younger sister were totally normal as well.

When I returned for my next meeting with Ron, he gave me another assignment.

"What's the only thing worse than believing you caused a fatal accident?" he asked.

I didn't know the answer he was looking for. What could be worse?

"Once your girls understand that they didn't cause the accident, you've got another issue you're going to need to address. Once they know that they didn't in any way bring about the accident, they'll also begin to realize that they had no control over anything that happened that afternoon, and they may start to wonder if they have any influence over *anything* that happens to them or to the people they care about." That's a profound fear for adults as well as children because it's based in so much truth. After all, it's better to feel overly responsible and guilty than out-of-control and totally helpless.

What can we control in this world full of chaos and violence? Not much, as it turns out. With that reality in mind, how can we keep from throwing up our hands in despair of having any positive impact in our lives and the lives of others? Ron helped me with this dilemma too, and in helping my children gain some reasonable sense of empowerment, I got a healthy dose myself.

We can't control the acts of nature or even the crazy driver in the next lane on the expressway, but there are a few areas where we have significant influence. We can wear seat belts; we can follow the speed limit and traffic laws; we can drive sober, alert, and with the cell phone out of reach. We can elect not to smoke. We can exercise regularly and eat a healthier diet. In doing these simple things, we positively influence our own health and the health of our families. We can elect not to drink alcohol or to consume it only in moderation. We can elect not to use illegal drugs and to be responsible in our use of prescription medications. I took the girls with me when I scheduled my first appointments for mammograms and the dreaded colonoscopies! I explained what I was doing and why. I was being proactive about guarding my health, and I wanted them to do the same thing. So much in our lives is beyond our control, but we can have some impact. We don't have to behave like sheep led to slaughter.

Beyond personal health, we also have a responsibility to our communities and to our environment. As the girls got older, we discussed why it is so important to vote, especially in local and state elections, and we talked about which companies we wanted to patronize and which ones we needed to boycott. One person can make a difference, and to paraphrase Margaret Mead, a small group of concerned, responsible people can make all the difference in the world. In the closing chapter of his book *Collapse*, author David Jared offered me tremendous hope by arguing that informed consumers who vote at the ballot box, with their pocketbooks, and with their stockholder proxy cards can have a considerable impact on the environmental policy decisions of even the largest multinational corporations. He'd seen it happen several times in researching his book, and I was delighted at the thought of having all that power for good.

Sometimes I worry if I've created a monster by telling my daughters how much impact and responsibility they have as consumers, and their youth minister with her strong sense of social justice has reinforced everything I've told them. One of my daughters won't wear anything from certain clothing manufacturers because she thinks the items may have been produced with child labor or in sweatshop conditions. She won't darken the door of any coffeehouse unless they sell fair-trade coffee, and she refuses factory-farmed meat of any kind because she knows how much water and grain it takes to produce a pound of hamburger. I'm not as good a steward of the earth as my girls are. But whenever I'm tempted to shake my head at my daughters' activism, I remind myself that their idealism is hope paired with action, and their actions honor the legacy of their sister's life. Virginia wanted to be outside all the time, and she kept a beaten-up pencil box, which she dubbed her "nature box," full of sticks, rocks, dead bugs, and lichens. Every time we went in the backyard, she wanted to add to her collection of flora and fauna. If Virginia had lived, I think she would have been very green in her lifestyle choices as an adult, and I suspect that somewhere, somehow, she is applauding her sisters' choices. That is my moment of magical thinking, and it brings me great joy.

Obviously, one of the most important ways we can serve our communities and our faith is through charitable work. Whether you're taking a meal to a neighbor who has just had a baby, hammering nails on a Habitat for Humanity house, or picking up trash near a local stream, everything you do to "pay it forward" and make your sphere of influence safer, cleaner, and kinder improves the lives of everyone you touch.

As I wrote this book, I wanted to be especially careful not to write anything that would be hurtful or offensive to Daniel. He had already been through enough pain for five lifetimes. As I finished the manuscript, though, my focus shifted. How would what I had written impact my surviving daughters? The thought of hurting them again was inconceivable, so I sent them the manuscript with full rights of censorship! While revisiting the accident and their sister's death was difficult for them, they were completely supportive of the book. In fact, I got a bonus. One of my daughters wrote me an e-mail—a letter to bereaved parents from a surviving child. Her insights were so poignant and her advice so salient that I knew I had to include her letter in the manuscript.

Mom,

In your chapter on magical thinking and approaching the lost child's siblings, you might want to add something about counseling as an option for the surviving children. They may not be interested, and it will depend on their ages and the situation, but they may benefit greatly from counseling also.

Every surviving sibling will experience the loss differently. The kind of relationship your children had with each other before the loss may have an immense bearing on how the children grieve and how they perceive themselves. For some, it will be the equivalent of losing a best friend, and it will be truly traumatic. Some may feel very distant from the event, and the real hardship for them will be watching the rest of their family grieve and not knowing what they are supposed to do or how they are supposed to feel. (I think part of the reason magical thinking was such a big part of my own experience was because I was so jealous of Virginia, although it was difficult for me to remember and admit to having felt that way.)

Your children may struggle with how other people expect them to react, and they may well have ample material for their own top ten lists. (In my case, I not only suffered from a lot of magical thinking, but I felt very guilty for not "crying enough" or "missing her enough." I also didn't want to talk about what had happened because I got frustrated with the assumptions people would make.) If adults can be tactless and overly curious, you can only imagine what other kids and teenagers might say to your kids. Plus, what are the people who are there to "watch the house burn" saying to your surviving kids?

Parents should know that, depending on the circumstances of the loss of their child, their other children may never be the same, and it may take years before they are truly able to understand and process what has happened to them and their family. They will grieve and heal on a very different timeline, and their experiences will affect their outlook and their relationships into adulthood, though they may not realize it. Ask them how they feel, but give them the space to answer honestly and know that they are entitled to feel the whole spectrum of emotions, from anger and sorrow to confusion and even boredom. They are on their own journey of grief and healing, self-discovery, and growing up.

As difficult as it is to be a grieving parent, it is also difficult to be the child of a grieving parent. It can be scary and hard for kids, especially young kids, to see their parents crying. You shouldn't have to cover up your grief, but try to get the support you need to be able to support your surviving children if they need it. Likewise, your children may try to do anything they can to make you smile or laugh—after all, they love you! It's hard for them to see you sad, and they need to smile and laugh too! You have a right to smile and laugh even if you are still sad. Let them know that they still make you happy, that you appreciate them, and that they are important to you, even if you feel that you have been drained of energy, patience, and grace. Their lives are not over, even if you have moments in which you feel like yours is.

It is just as bad for them to feel guilty about causing the death or causing you pain as it is for them to feel that there is nothing they can do to engage with you or bring you happiness or relief from your sorrow. Your surviving kids can't fix your grief or make it go away, but don't stop enjoying having them in your life. They shouldn't feel pressured to entertain you or be your sole source of happiness, but they need to know that they are a positive and appreciated part of your life.

Not all children will feel this way, but some of them may feel that with so much emphasis being placed on the child who has died, they have ceased to be important or have become invisible. They may feel resentful toward their lost sibling or even become frightened of ghosts or think that their dead sibling is watching them or can punish them. (You could think of this as "voodoo thinking"—a whole step beyond magical thinking!) Some of them may desperately crave attention, especially if they were attention seekers before. For some of them, the change in day-to-day life may be so significant that they feel as if they have lost their parents as well as a brother or sister.

As a grieving parent, you may not have the emotional resources to provide all of the answers and support your child needs, which is another reason counseling may be helpful to both you and your child. But you can provide affirmation, even if it isn't verbal—hugs can say a lot.

It must be doubly hard to be the parent of a child who has died and the parent of a child who is grieving or who is overwhelmed by the grief of others. But the surviving children still need you. If you need help packing lunches, doing laundry, or driving carpool, try to get it. Some children need to get back to the routine they're used to in order to cope, but some of them may need a whole new routine altogether.

It will be hard for your kids to see each other grieve, and it will probably be hard for you to watch them grieve, but keep in mind that you cannot protect them from everything. They are going to experience fear, sorrow, confusion, anger, and regret. Don't try to deny that something is wrong, but let them enjoy their favorite activities if they want to. Don't let them feel afraid to have fun again around you. You may not have the time or the energy to do everything with them, but you can let trusted family members and friends spend time with them and do fun activities together if your kids express interest. They need time to process their emotions, and they also need a break from those emotions. It will be hard to create a place of balance for them, but make it your goal.

Your kids may want to distract themselves with things like television, the Internet, books, and video games. Let them enjoy these things in moderation, especially if it helps your kids feel like they are living normally again, but be careful not to let them withdraw or shut themselves off from reality. Creative outlets— things like journaling, drawing and painting, building models, playing games, and making crafts—are a good way for your kids to entertain themselves, have fun, and express their emotions at the same time.

Keep in mind that your children could feel singled out in school; they may feel that they are different or that something is wrong with them. It can be hard for them to know what to say to their friends or how to answer questions. They may even be tempted to milk their situation for all it's worth and use it to get attention or feel special! Talk to your kids' teachers, or if it is too difficult for you, have a close friend or minister approach them on your behalf. Your kids should know that whether they want to talk about their experience or not is their choice, and they should feel that they can trust the adults they spend time with.

As your kids get older, certain parts of their experience of grief will blur and other parts will come into focus. They may experience flashbacks. Things will connect and become significant in ways they didn't before. This is part of the different timeline. Your healing experience will continue for the rest of your life, and so will theirs.

I am exhausted and I need to go to bed, but I wanted to send this along.

I love you so much. I'll talk to you tomorrow,

Love, Anna

To have daughters who can write like this . . . surely I am one of the luckiest women on the planet!

Chapter Nine

BIRTHDAYS, HOLIDAYS, AND ORDINARY TUESDAYS

"What we need are not new horizons.
What we need are fresh eyes
with which to see the horizons already before us."
—Marcel Proust

Special occasions change forever after the loss of a child. Every holiday, anniversary, and birthday will be tinged with sadness. That isn't to say that you won't experience plenty of joy and laughter with your friends and family again. You'll have fun again, and you'll let the little things get on your nerves again while you're wrapping Christmas packages or cleaning up the huge mess in the kitchen after a holiday meal. But you will look forward to family gatherings in a way you never have before. You will develop an insight, a love, and a sense of perspective that only the people who have endured great sorrow can have. Each holiday will be filled with more poignancy and significance.

You'll need to start some new holiday traditions to help your family heal and move on, but as you already know, for the first year or two you won't feel like doing much of anything. I wanted to keep hanging Virginia's Christmas stocking on the mantle for the first couple of years after her death, but Daniel wisely counseled me not to do that. Virginia was celebrating Christmas in a different place, and I had to accept that fact. I think it's important to remember your child at holidays with some gesture. If it isn't too painful, talking about past celebrations with your child can trigger the best memories. Be mindful of your spouse's stage of grief in these circumstances, though, and be especially compassionate. I was hungry to talk about Virginia and all of her mischief and antics during the holidays, and my daughters seemed to enjoy these funny conversations too, but Daniel wasn't ready. These conversations made him silent and sad, which in turn upset my older girls. It wasn't worth it. I learned to reserve talking about Virginia like this for the times when I was alone with my daughters or when I was with close friends.

For several years after Virginia's death, I took balloons and Barbie dolls to the grave site on her birthday, and I replaced the silk flowers in the memorial urn every few months. On the first anniversary of Virginia's death, my older daughters' Girl Scout troop and their parents helped me prepare a meal for the families staying at the nearby Ronald McDonald House. I felt so much love from these women and their daughters, and once again, I thought it was a terrific way to celebrate the legacy of Virginia's life.

You'll find your own way to honor your child's memory. Some practices will become traditions; others will change over time. And if for the first few years you don't have the energy or the spirit to do anything, that's all right, too. In fact, it's more than all right—you must do what works for you.

At first, I expected my grief to be at its worst on the actual holidays and milestones. What I found, though, was that the anticipation of the holiday was usually much more painful than the actual day. Most of the bereaved parents I've talked with have said the same thing. You'll likely find some relief from your pain on the days you expect it to be the worst. Grief gets me when I'm not looking, when I'm not prepared—it's a sucker punch to my soul. Grief hits me on the ordinary Tuesday when I'm in the grocery store and I see a little girl who looks like Virginia. Grief gets me when I hear a radio or TV report about another automobile accident that has taken a child's life. Grief gets me when I turn to page A4 or A6 of *The New York Times* and read the names of six or eight more young men and women who have died fighting in Iraq or Afghanistan.

I don't like to grieve in public, but some people find it cathartic, and I'll never stand in judgment of what helps them. And sometimes grief doesn't give you much choice. One of the worst episodes I had happened about eighteen months after Virginia died. I had gone to Target to pick up some last-minute items for a Christmas luncheon that the women in my church were hosting. I saw a young mother with a four- or five-year-old little blonde cherub sitting in the front of her shopping cart. The little girl was chattering away, and her curly hair reminded me so much of Virginia's, it was eerie. When the little girl asked her mom if they could go look at the Barbie dolls in the toy section, I lost it. I totally disintegrated. I started crying, and I couldn't stop. My heart was racing, and I felt my face and neck flush. I left my shopping cart right in the middle of the aisle, and I ran out to my car as fast as I could. I sobbed all the way as I drove back to my church, and I stumbled to the church's kitchen door, blabbering like a fool, apologizing for not bringing the tablecloths or candles or whatever it was I had been sent to get. Two of the older women in our congregation, one a widow and one a grandmother who had lost a grandson, met me at the door, hugged me, and let me cry.

Neighborhood swim meets got me, too. I went to see my other daughters compete, and of course I also saw the little ones, the kids Virginia's age, growing taller and stronger every season. I watched them climb onto the diving blocks for the first time, learn to do flip turns, and skip over to collect their ribbons. Sometimes I watched with joy, but other evenings I had to walk away for a little while until it was time for the older girls' events. Virginia learned to swim early, and she loved to flirt with the college-aged boy who came home from Villanova in the summer to coach the youngest kids. What a shame Virginia never got to learn to do those flip turns; never got a chance to spring off those diving blocks. What a shame.

Prepare yourself for those events where you're going to feel your child's absence most acutely, and prepare yourself for the holidays. Remember and honor the memory of your child, but make some new traditions too. Your holidays should be celebrations even if those celebrations are always tinged with sadness. Give yourself some time; be gentle with yourself. Planning new traditions will be easier after the first two or three years of your loss. Accept that grief will hit you and hit you hard, often in places and at times when you least expect it and are least prepared. As time passes, though, those episodes will be farther and farther apart and less intense. Memory will bring you more joy and less pain every season.

Chapter Ten

THE TRANSFORMATION

*"We must accept finite disappointment,
but we must never lose infinite hope."*
—Martin Luther King, Jr.

A year from now, you won't recognize yourself.

As you work through your grief, you will be fundamentally changed as a person. Most of the people I've known who have resolved their grief are stronger, more determined, and more insightful than they ever dreamed they would be. Yet, I know every one of us would trade every bit of that new strength for just one more day with the children we lost. Ah, that we could! This newfound confidence is no consolation—but it is an asset for you, and one you will grow to appreciate.

No one told me how radically I would change as I went through the grieving process. I wish someone had. Natalie, a woman from my church, lost her son in a drowning accident about three years after Virginia's death. We walked around the trails at Atlanta's Chastain Park on a couple of mornings, and Natalie talked about her little boy and all the pain and all the guilt. I told her, on the mornings we walked and each time I saw her at church, that she would be a different person within eighteen months. She'd give me a wan smile and no reply. Her pain was still too raw for her to see beyond the next day. By the next spring, though, Natalie and her husband had filled in the pool where their son drowned, and they had bought another house that they were renovating. Natalie was pregnant with a new baby. She had sloughed off most of the irrational guilt she felt about her son's accident, and she and her husband had plans underway to build a playground and a park as a memorial to the son they had lost.

"Betsy," she said later, "when you told me last year I'd be so much different and so much stronger, I couldn't even grasp what you were saying, In fact, it irritated me. But now I get it. I am tougher and more capable than I was."

Once again, this is no consolation—a skill and a strength certainly, but it doesn't begin to compensate for what you have lost. Losing a child forces us to reexamine everything in our lives: our work, our priorities, our relationships, and our faith. False platitudes and superficial people become intolerable to us, and we become acutely aware of how important it is to live in the present and enjoy every minute we have with the people we love. We develop a deeper clarity about what is important and what is trivial. I feel much greater compassion for people in pain, both emotional and physical, than I did before I lost Virginia.

I have lost most of my patience, however, with whiners and people who let small, insignificant issues take up significant time in their lives or conversations. A college buddy of mine was complaining bitterly at a girl's-night-out dinner about a contractor who had delivered the wrong color of brick for her new patio. She went on and on about the problem for what seemed like an hour. I finally grew so disgusted that I got up and left the table for a few minutes. This leads me to another issue that you may already be experiencing: your circle of friends is likely to change significantly over the next few years as you heal. It's sad to watch some of those old friendships diminish or fall away completely, but as you change and grow, you'll find a need to fill your life with people of greater depth and introspection.

My neighbor lost her brother and her father in an automobile accident when she was still in grade school. One of her favorite quotes (but one she won't take credit for) is, "I don't care too much about being friends with someone unless life has kicked the s--- out of them, and they've had the courage to get up and kick back." Life certainly kicked this woman. The accident that killed her father and her brother was supposed to cripple her for life; initially, her doctors didn't think she'd walk again, but she got back up and walked, literally and metaphorically. She did all the painful work of physical therapy she needed to do, and she put in the time and pain to get her journalism degree from Vanderbilt. She later won a Pulitzer Prize for the investigative work she did as a reporter for *The Wall Street Journal.* Courage is her trademark, and I will always be grateful to her for the time she gave my daughters, talking to them about how it feels to lose a sibling and how hard it is to watch your parents grieve.

I felt isolated for a while after Virginia's death, isolated from people I'd thought would be a greater source of support. Later, as I heard their comments, I understood their absence. They told mutual friends they simply didn't know what to say to me. Conversations had become difficult and stilted. In trying to talk to me about what they considered to be their more mundane issues and problems, they felt guilty or even shallow. I felt sad and lonely when I first heard these things, but after a short while, I began to understand what they were feeling. My family's pain was too big for them to incorporate into their own lives. It was, after all, *my* pain to deal with, not theirs. Suddenly it was okay; I felt no bitterness toward them. I let them slip away.

I was beginning a metamorphosis. I was incorporating my grief into a new, stronger sense of self. I was moving into a place of acceptance of my life without Virginia. I was far sadder, but far wiser too. You are changing as well—beginning to embrace the reality of your life and your future without your child. After about a year in the grieving process, you'll realize you have a choice. You can elect to let your grief crush you or you can get up again, look outward, and decide to go forward. What would your child want you to do? And when you die, how do you want your friends and family to react? Reengaging in life is hard, but unless we do it, we wither and die as well.

Chapter Eleven

WATCHING THE HOUSE BURN

"I measure every grief I meet with narrow, probing eyes.
I wonder if it weighs like mine or has an easier size."

—Emily Dickinson

What is the dark shard in the human spirit that makes us rubberneck at the sight of an automobile accident or hurry to watch a house fire or the funnel cloud of a tornado? A few individuals I know can't bear to look at accidents or violence of any sort, but most people, whether they'll admit it or not, are fascinated at some level by violence and destruction.

The same disturbing part of our nature that rivets our attention to the flames and the gunfire on the nightly news also drove people to ask question after question about the details of Virginia's accident and death. I was unnerved by how early and how much people asked me; I couldn't imagine asking a grieving parent the sorts of questions I fielded.

I think, for the vast majority of those people, their need to know was motivated by their own fear. They seemed fascinated and horrified at "watching the house burn" because they realized that it could have just as easily been their own house . . . or their own child.

The more involved you are in your church, your neighborhood, or your child's school, the more love and support you'll probably find as you grieve. Unfortunately, along with that support, you'll also find that a handful of people will come to watch the house burn and observe your suffering, whether they are conscious of it or not. The love and support of the many far outweighs the prying eyes of the one or two, but I want you to be prepared for those prying eyes and ready to protect yourself and your family.

As I mentioned before, we were lucky enough to have our friends and neighbors and the families from our church bring us meals for over a month after the accident. I wanted to thank everyone who brought food, but some days I had counseling appointments or follow-up doctor's appointments for my older children, and some days I was simply too exhausted physically or emotionally to talk to anyone. A mother from Virginia's preschool made an excellent suggestion. She had just lost a family member, and she recognized that on some days as you grieve you will need company and support, and on some days you will need quiet and solitude. This wise woman encouraged us to put a large cooler out by our garage door with a note that read, "Thank you so much for bringing this meal. If the garage door is up, please come in and visit if you'd like. If the garage door is down, please understand that the family is resting or praying and they need privacy."

As you already know, grieving takes tremendous emotional and physical energy, and putting on your game face time after time to field questions or simply to show hospitality may strain you past the breaking point. Grieve on your own terms and in your own time. If you don't want to see people or talk, don't. Wait until you feel stronger. Obviously, you don't want to be rude to people or dismiss their sympathy, but you do have to be realistic about how much social time you can sustain, and you have to buffer yourself and your family from too much company and scrutiny. Try the technique with the garage-door cooler; it worked beautifully.

Give yourself plenty of time—several months or even a year—but if you find yourself deliberately isolating from friends and family on a regular basis after that time period, discuss it with your counselor. You want to make sure depression isn't causing you to withdraw from the people who love and care about you most. I felt the need to disengage and be quiet, to pray, to meditate, and to reenergize myself. I was licking my wounds so that I could go out into the world again and function. Remember, even Christ had to withdraw from the crowds to pray and re-center from time to time. Taking the time for introspection is healthy and a critical part of the overall healing process. It's all a matter of balance, and with good counsel you'll know if you're holding that balance or spending too much time alone.

A woman with whom I'd taught Sunday school called a couple of weeks after Virginia's death and said, "Well, Bets, do I still have to handle you with kid gloves? And have you been run over by the steam-roller of Christian compassion?" I laughed out loud, and it felt so good to laugh. Yes, we had been overrun. We felt loved and supported . . . and exhausted. One lady from our congregation called on the phone or came by the house nearly every day for two weeks, and she talked incessantly. We hadn't even been particularly close friends with her before the accident. She got on my nerves so badly, I thought I would explode, but Daniel was able to handle her with much more grace. We had a tacit agreement that whenever this kind-but-tiring soul came to visit, I would escape upstairs and Dan would entertain her for a few minutes before excusing himself to check on our children or me. If you can, talk to your spouse and other family members about these predicaments before they begin to wear you down so that you can try to work out some type of solution.

I had a thought-provoking conversation with my minister not too long after Virginia's death. He said, "Betsy, you need to let down and let others wash your feet. Let people do things for you instead of feeling that you have to be strong and 'on' at all times. People want to help you, and you'll do them a service if you allow yourself to accept that help." I was right in the middle of the conservation-and-withdrawal phase of my grief at that time, and I was direct to the point of being rude in my response to him. I told my minister that I needed to grieve in my own way, and that it was not my job to make others feel good about themselves at that point in my life. Frankly, I was angry at his comment (of course, I was angry about everything). It wasn't until years later when another counselor recommended that I read Hendrix and Hunt's excellent book on relationships, *Receiving Love*, that I finally understood what my minister had been trying to tell me. I had always been a hyper-responsible person. I had always believed that if work was going to get done, I was better off to do it all myself than to ask for help. I was the nurturer and caregiver in my family and always had been. I was extremely uncomfortable being the vulnerable one—I saw it as a sign of weakness and loss of control to accept help from other people. I didn't want to let go.

Only through losing Virginia and experiencing the slow process of healing have I finally realized that my constant need to be in control and show self-control was a selfish posture and a lonely way to live. To have the healthiest relationships with others and the strongest connection to God, we have to admit when we need help and be willing to accept that help when it comes our way. Admission and acceptance require grace; they are surrender, and if you are like me, it may take you years to find your way toward that goal. But when you do, you will realize the ultimate paradox: in admitting our weakness, we are strengthened. In accepting love and help, we are empowered and able to love and care for others more fully. Let the angels minister to you when they come along—it is the best thing for both of you.

Chapter Twelve

HEALTHY COPING

"The only cure for grief is action."
—George Henry Lewis

*"The truth is that our finest moments are most likely to occur
when we are feeling deeply unhappy. For it is only in such moments,
propelled by our discomfort, that we are likely to step out of our ruts and
start searching for different, better ways and truer answers."*
—M. Scott Peck

When my internist insisted that we start getting some physical exercise as soon as possible after Virginia's death, she set me up for a lifestyle change that has had a tremendous positive impact on my health. I had run and played a poor excuse for tennis in college and before my kids were born, but with three children, a part-time job, and a slew of volunteer obligations at church and at the girls' schools, I seldom made time to work out.

Once Virginia died, though, I started walking. I started walking and talking and crying with old college roommates and friends from my neighborhood. The walking helped me emotionally; it helped tremendously. Virginia died in April, and in August I began running with a woman who had recently lost her father to suicide. We had plenty to talk about as we ran. Running helped me feel even better psychologically than walking. Dan protested that all this running was going to ruin my knees and ankles, but I invested in a good pair of running shoes, and I iced my knees with bags of frozen peas. The more I ran, the better I felt, and I ran my first 5K on New Year's Eve that year. I celebrated later with my running partner and several of my neighbors who had also finished the race. The following summer I ran in Atlanta's famous Peachtree Road Race 10K, and by the next Thanksgiving I was ready for the city's half marathon.

The time I spent training and running soon became a point of contention between Daniel and me, but the endorphins I felt after a long run couldn't be mimicked by any other form of exercise or any pharmaceutical. I was and still am a very slow runner—I dubbed myself "The Queen of the Eleven-Minute Mile." But my pace didn't matter at all. I was out nearly every morning running. I felt stronger, and I was finishing races. For the first time in my life I was fit.

This may all sound a little silly, but it's true, and it has application to you: if you can find a constructive or creative activity that helps you as you grieve, then by all means do it. My mother-in-law immersed herself in the work of her family business after her own son's death, and she told me that the productivity of work gave her some relief from her suffering. Some people will say that by engaging in these sorts of activities you are hiding from your grief, but I disagree. I don't think there is anywhere under the sun, physically or emotionally, where you can hide for long from the pain of losing a child. If work, running, painting, or fly-fishing gives you some solace, then work, run, paint, or fish like crazy for a while.

You've probably already considered the use of antidepressants in the grieving process. This is a personal decision that you should make with the help of your spouse, your physician, and your counselor. You should have the final say. Dan, as I mentioned before, was against the use of antidepressants for himself and for me for very legitimate reasons, and he discouraged me from taking them even after our internist prescribed them. He was concerned that my taking the medication would mask the pain of the grieving process and actually make it more difficult for me to cope and heal in the long run. I took the medication, a serotonin reuptake inhibitor (SSRI), against his wishes.

Within two weeks of starting the medication, I was able to tell a big difference in the way I felt. I still grieved and cried nearly every day, but I no longer felt like I was slipping off the edge of the world into a depression from which I couldn't climb out. I had an emotional floor beneath which I didn't sink, and suddenly I felt stronger and more assertive in my dealings with other people. I could calmly and rationally answer Daniel's challenges about why I was taking the medication in the first place. I didn't have sobbing fits anymore. I still got angry with some of the things people said and did, but I didn't overreact and fly into blind rages as I had in the past. Coping with my grief became easier. Coping with everything and everyone in general became easier. I found my sense of humor and sense of irony in situations where earlier I had been morose. And for the first time since Virginia's death, I was able to quiet my mind long enough to meditate and pray.

There was a side benefit to this as well: with the help of counseling and the balancing effects of the SSRI, I was able to break a destructive pattern that had hampered me since I was a teenager. Throughout my life I had been taught that conflict was to be avoided at all costs, and that any expression of anger or unpleasantness was unacceptable. Naturally, when I became an adult, if something in my business or personal life hurt or irritated me, I would just "let it go." I stuffed down my anger for months at a time until some small incident or comment triggered my temper. At that point I would either sob uncontrollably or fall into fits of rage. I'd be so embarrassed that I'd lost control over such a minor issue that I would apologize profusely for the outburst, never addressing the mounting problems that had gotten me so angry in the first place. I'd redouble my efforts to "let things go" and promise myself and Dan that such explosions would never happen again. The whole cycle would begin again with the same unpleasant and useless outcome. Now, ironically, after only a few months of my daughter's death, I was able to more clearly and calmly articulate my feelings and needs. I could say what I was thinking in a direct way. It was a radical change.

The medication was hardly a panacea, though. I felt drowsy and lethargic, especially late in the afternoons, and I gained over ten pounds in a year. All those stories you hear about SSRIs blunting sex drive and orgasm are true too. Antidepressants, no matter what the mode of action in the nervous system, can be effective tools to help many people cope with grief—but they are only one set of tools. They all have side effects, and relying only on these medications isn't the way to go. Medication had to be paired with exercise, counseling, the support of friends, the passage of time, and most importantly, faith in order to play a critical role in my healing. I don't know that any one of these things alone would have been enough.

A couple of years after Virginia died, my internist retired to spend more time with her children. My new physician said that he would continue to prescribe the antidepressants for me, but only if I was actively involved in counseling as well. I thought that was a sound approach. As time went by, new SSRIs with better side-effect profiles came on the market. I still take a low dose of the medication every other day. One strong word of caution: don't ever stop taking antidepressants suddenly. I had the flu not too long after I started taking the medication, and I couldn't keep anything on my stomach. Even after I was able to eat and drink again, I didn't resume taking my medication right away. I never felt suicidal, but the depression and the helplessness I felt were unlike anything I had ever experienced before. I was struggling to get up and get through the routine of the day, and while I know that some of what I was feeling was weakness from the flu, I also believe that part of my emotional nosedive was caused by my quick withdrawal from the medication. When I go back and read some of the things I wrote during those few days, I get alarmed. *Darkness* is not a strong enough word. When you feel it is time to change or stop taking medications of this kind (or long-term medications of any sort, for that matter), talk to your doctor. Titrate down slowly—in other words, work with your physician and decrease your dosage gradually.

There's another facet to healthy coping: pray. For the first few weeks after Virginia died, my head was reeling, and I couldn't quiet my mind enough to pray at all. A friend of my daughters gave us a CD of music played on a Native American flute. I would listen to the CD throughout the week, sitting quietly with my eyes closed. The music soothed me and helped me feel centered again. Later, I started praying out loud anywhere I could—in the car in the notorious Atlanta traffic, in the shower, in the kitchen while I was preparing meals. The more I prayed, the easier and more natural it became. And the easier it became, the more effective it became. People who saw me praying out loud while I sat in traffic on the expressway must have thought I was loony, and of course I was, but in that time of prayer, I was more hopeful and more lucid than at any other time of the day. Some friends of ours belong to a Marionite Catholic Church, and they sent me a letter telling me that a forty-day Mass was being said for Virginia. I was so touched and comforted by the fact that somewhere out there someone was praying continuously for the spirit of my daughter.

I've even had "Joan of Arc" experiences in prayer twice since Virginia died. I didn't experience anything nearly as dramatic as St. Joan's divine instructions about leading the French army into battle, but spiritually these experiences have been the most profound of my life. The first time it happened, I was crying in the shower, begging God to bring Virginia back and give me some relief from my pain. I rested my head against the shower tile, and a voice inside my brain clearly answered, "Lean on me. I am here with you. I am here with you, and I will not let you fall." The sense of comfort and compassion I felt at that moment still carries me. Nearly two years later, I was praying in church about a presentation I had to make in front of a group of elders concerning the construction of a nature walk on our church grounds in memory of several children in our congregation who had died. I was afraid I would be too nervous to speak or that I would break down and cry before I finished the presentation. The same voice I'd heard at my lowest point of grief two years earlier spoke to me again in the church pew and said, "Trust me. I will give you a voice." He did. The whole presentation went better than I ever could have imagined.

I'm sold on the power of prayer. Whether God is speaking to us directly or is reordering the firing of neurons and neurotransmitters in our cortex, it doesn't matter. Something astonishing happens in the human brain when we pray and meditate, and today neuroscientists are able to observe those changes in electrical activity in the cerebrum through functional MRIs and PET (Positron Emission Tomography) scans. I had the chance to see some early recordings of PET scans when I was in graduate school. At that time we were watching the changes in electrical activity in the higher learning centers of children when they were read the same stories over and over again. The results were astonishing. (If your child wants to read *Goodnight Moon* five times a night every evening for a month, do it—you are knitting powerful neural connections for them as you read that bedtime story!). I am convinced that after we pray and meditate, we can cope more effectively with stress and see patterns and solutions to problems more clearly. And the more we pray, the more helpful it becomes. If you'd like to see the visual documentation of how the brain changes during prayer, Google "positron emission tomography (or PET) during prayer" to see what the prayer professionals, Franciscan nuns and Tibetan Buddhist priests displayed cortically in several different research studies.[9] I think you'll be astounded and uplifted. I was.

The positive impact of taking a vacation while you're grieving may seem insignificant or shallow compared with the importance of prayer or counseling, but getting away from it all for a few days truly can help. Daniel and I took the girls and his mom to the beach for a week the summer after Virginia died. One of my daughters still had the pins in her femur from her surgery and it was hard for her to walk, but the trip was worth it. We did our share of grieving and crying, but being in a beautiful place where we could see and hear the ocean was soothing. I also made my first stab at yoga during that trip, and my unbalanced attempts at some of the poses were hilarious; my mother-in-law and I couldn't stop laughing. We needed to laugh.

One afternoon the girls and I wandered around the shops near the beach, and a couple of the sales clerks commented on how cute the twins were. They asked me if I had any other children. Get ready for that question, and have an answer prepared. I said, "Yes, I have another little girl who is five, but she's not with us today." I didn't want to tell our story to people I knew I'd never see again, and they didn't need to be assaulted with the circumstances of our grief. The answer I gave the clerks that day seemed to satisfy everyone, including the twins. One of the girls confided to me, "Mom, it's nice not to have to be the sad family for just a little while, isn't it?" She was ten years old. The wisdom of children, eh? As you move forward in your life, you'll meet more and more people who don't know your story. What you tell strangers and casual acquaintances will naturally be far different from what you share with close friends.

Your faith, counseling, support from friends and family, your work or your creative outlets—you've got dozens of tools at your disposal to help you work through your grief as fully and in as healthy a way as possible. Be gentle and patient with yourself, though. You may know intellectually that you have access to all these great tools, but emotionally you may not have the energy to use them on a consistent basis for the first several months. That's okay—they are there when you are ready.

Chapter Thirteen

BIZARRE BEHAVIORS

"No man was ever so much deceived by another as by himself."
—Greville

"I did not fall from grace, I dove."
—Sue Monk Kidd, *The Mermaid Chair*

Sue Monk Kidd's quote sums up my experience exactly. I didn't know whether to laugh or cry when I read her book. As you read this chapter, you should know that this was the most difficult chapter for me to construct, because writing it forced me to openly admit some of the most destructive, selfish, and downright stupid things I have ever done. I could try to blame all my mistakes (yeah, go ahead and call them what they are—sins) on my grief or on some sort of temporary insanity, but I would be lying to myself and to you. My decision-making abilities were certainly damaged, and my judgment skills were impaired in my grief, but in the end, at a fundamental level, I knew that what I was doing was wrong.

Even under the most difficult circumstances, we almost always have free will and choice. I can never go back and correct the mistakes that I've made, and I can't undo the hurt I caused so many people, especially my own children. When mistakes are serious enough, and mine certainly were, even the best intentions and efforts won't be enough to let you atone.

The shame I feel at times about the things I did during that awful period is nearly as overwhelming as the grief I felt in the early days after I lost Virginia. You don't ever want to find yourself in that spiritual and emotional position. As they say in the popular vernacular, *it sucks.* I'm grateful every day that I'm counting on God's forgiveness and grace and not the grace of humanity to get me through life, because I have a handful of former friends who will no longer speak to me. I'm afraid they are lost to me forever; I don't know that they will ever be able to forgive me. The key is for me to be able to forgive myself. I'm working on it.

In doing research for another book, I came across the work of a psychologist named John Preston. Preston describes clearly and accurately what happens to individuals when they are exposed to severe stress for prolonged periods of time. Even the healthiest personalities are more likely to show maladaptive behavior in those situations, and if you stir a few mild neuroses into the stew (which, let's face it, most of us have), then the regression is even more pronounced and long-lasting. In this situation, it takes longer for the stressed individual to return to his or her baseline coping level.[10] I'm not suggesting that all grieving parents are going to act as though they have post-traumatic stress disorder or borderline personality disorder, but you do need to realize that your discernment and decision-making abilities may be significantly impacted while you're grieving, and you'll need to be especially mindful about your choices and your judgment for quite a while.

In the later stages of my grief, I acted in a way that ruined my marriage and several close friendships. As I said before, I had wonderful support in my grief from my friends, my neighbors, and the people in my church, but within my extended family and in my marriage I felt isolated. My counselor nailed it when he said, "Emotionally, you are starving to death." But when you're starving, you need to ask for help; you need to ask, even beg, for bread. Stealing is never okay, literally or emotionally.

I've never been a perfect parent by any stretch of the imagination, and I made countless mistakes raising my girls, but I was loving and present. As I was grieving, I became viciously critical of parents I considered less capable than myself. *Look at the kind of parent I was, and look at what happened to my adorable little girl,* I raged. These people who weren't paying attention, who weren't taking care of their kids . . . well, in my estimation they didn't deserve those children. And the people who didn't appreciate their spouses and families? In my warped view of reality, those men and women might as well have left expensive bicycles out in the rain to rust, and if someone else wanted to come along and claim those bicycles, clean them up, and take them home, then that was perfectly okay. In my disordered thinking processes, I believed I could make up my own rules for boundaries and morality for myself and for friends whom I thought had been wronged. That way of living doesn't work too well, trust me! Willfully disobeying God's directions for our lives will always lead to heartache.

As progressive, well-educated people, it's hard for most of us to visualize Satan as some cloven-hoofed demon hopping around behind our backs goading us to do evil, but I know that when we are emotionally and spiritually distraught, we are much more likely to engage in behaviors that are self-destructive or harmful to the people we love most. Your resolve and your reasoning are going to be as compromised as your physical immune system when you're grieving, and you need to surround yourself with people who love you enough to keep you healthy and accountable.

Ultimately, you are responsible for your own actions and choices, but you can count on the fact that you'll be much more vulnerable to abusing drugs and alcohol while you're grieving, and you'll be much more vulnerable to entering bad relationships or being exploited. Protect yourself. As Christ told his disciples, "I am sending you out into a world of wolves; therefore, be as wily as serpents and as gentle as doves" (Matthew 10:16). You'll need to focus on being wily for quite some time.

In the Beaux-Arts Museum in Montreal, in a small nondescript gallery on the third floor, there is a piece of sculpture encased in a glass cabinet about three feet tall. In the case is a bronze casting of an old man—thin, wiry, and wearing medieval tights and battered shoes. His face is partially obscured by a hood, and his arms are wrapped tightly around his emaciated body as if to protect himself from the cold. The sculpture was cast by Jacques-Louis Gautier in 1855, and it is entitled *Mephistopheles*. Every time I've walked by that diminutive statue, I've had a hard time looking away. I've taken my daughters and my youngest stepdaughter into that gallery, and they tell me that they have exactly the same reaction that I do to the sculpture. It is a dark magnet that pulls our gaze. While on the surface the old man seems frail and harmless, a closer look shows how tough, canny, and resilient this character is. He's been wandering the world for centuries; he's seen it all, and he's not going away. He is the embodiment of evil and cunning. Part of that old man is in your head and spirit, and part of that old man is in my head and spirit. Don't let him get the upper hand.

When I read science writer Ann Finkbeiner's book on the long-term effects of grief, *Living with Loss Through the Years,* I was appalled by the stories she related in several chapters about people who denied their children had ever existed or denied that they cared much at all about losing their sons or daughters. I read the book in the early weeks of my grief, and my initial response was to label these bereaved parents as mentally ill or completely soulless monsters. I shook my head in disgust at the chapter, "Janet Wright's Bad Friends." I hardly had the energy to brush my teeth and get a shower; the notion of sustaining an affair as Janet Wright did was beyond my comprehension. However, as the weeks rolled by, I learned quickly to stop passing judgment. I quit saying to myself, "I'm too good to think like those people or to even imagine doing what they did." I wasn't too good, and when I look back now, I can scarcely believe the things I said and did. People are capable of doing outrageous and destructive things when they're grieving. You're not going to be yourself for a while.

To protect yourself and your family from the fallout of grief, you'll need to be acutely aware of warning signals both internally and externally. While some of this advice might appear cynical, it's all true, and like tough counseling, hearing the painful truth upfront may save you from greater pain in the long run.

After my mother died, people cautioned my father not to move, sell his house, or make any significant personal or business decisions for at least a year. That's sound advice when you lose a child as well. (However, I have known several grieving couples who felt strongly that they needed to move after their child's death. Their house was too closely connected in their minds with the child's illness or with an accident or suicide that caused the death. In that situation, talk to your counselor, and be mindful of how a physical move in that first year might affect your other children. In the end, though, moving might be the best choice for you.)

Some of the people around you will receive tremendous gratification in helping you through the grief process, and while for the overwhelming majority of people this is an altruistic endeavor, you must guard yourself against what I call "White Knight Syndrome." A woman I interviewed, Leanna, was being counseled by her minister after her child died, and after several months of sessions, even this professionally trained and able man confused the sympathy he felt for this woman for romantic love. To the minister's credit, he confessed his feelings for her and helped her find another therapist immediately. This woman and her family also left the congregation and joined another church. This was certainly the most ethical way to address the situation, but how sad to lose your spiritual community on top of losing your child!

Be aware that you too may be open and vulnerable to white knights while you're grieving. A former Atlanta police lieutenant told me that it was quite common for women to call him expressing love (or something like it) after he investigated cases for them or got these women or their children out of danger. If you are a grieving mother and someone is taking care of you or your children financially, legally, or medically, you need to be on your guard. Anyone who cares for your child and shows you and that child compassion will strike a deep chord in your spirit. Even if you and your spouse have a good relationship, you can get confused about your feelings toward caregivers, and if your marriage is troubled, as so often is the case after couples lose children, you'll need to be doubly careful.

Not everyone will show the same integrity and restraint as the minister and the police officer did. If as a married person you *do* find yourself attracted to anyone who is helping you through the grief process or with practical matters after the death of your child, cut off your contact as soon as possible. If you can, tell your spouse what you're feeling, and discuss it in counseling. Don't beat yourself up for having these feelings, and don't be too harsh with your spouse if he or she is having the same issues. What you are feeling is a common response in the face of the upheaval you've experienced. Ask a close friend to keep you accountable as you cut off contact, but realize that the circle of people you can trust to be discreet in this situation is very, very small. It's infuriating that you should have to guard your flank as you grieve, but it's a reality you can't afford to ignore in these later stages.

Children are irreplaceable and certainly not interchangeable, but another bizarre behavior some grieving parents exhibit is trying to find solace from the loss of one child in the life of a new baby. While there is certainly *nothing* wrong in deciding to have more children after you've lost an older son or daughter, be sure to give yourself plenty of time to heal physically and emotionally before you try to get pregnant again. Your grief should not be the legacy of your new child's life. I was fascinated and horrified when I read the life story of the Surrealist artist Salvador Dali, who was named after his dead brother. Dali's parents urged him to take on his dead brother's identity completely. The world is the beneficiary of Dali's tortured genius, but when you look at some of the grotesque imagery of Dali's paintings, you have to wonder what kind of psychological anguish the artist suffered because of his parents' grief.

Waiting a while to heal before adopting a child makes sense for all the same reasons. A neighbor of mine lost her son in a drowning accident when the little boy was three. She and her husband had another child a few years later, and shortly thereafter they adopted two more children with special needs from third-world orphanages. Not only did this family have two older children and three toddlers at this point, they were also trying to homeschool the children with little outside support. It was a disaster. Be gentle with yourself and allow yourself to heal before you take on significant emotional and financial challenges. Have more children or adopt children if you feel it's the right thing for your family, but make sure you're doing it for the right reasons and at the right time.

Adoption is a wonderful and loving decision, but you also need to educate yourself about the challenges that many adopted children face, especially as they enter adolescence. The problems that many adopted children encounter seem to be present even if the children are adopted early, healthy, and from nurturing environments. You owe it to yourself, your other children, the adopted child, and your extended family to go into the adoption process with realistic expectations and preparations.[11]

The healing process is complex, and you'll see fundamental shifts in your attitudes and behavior especially in the later stages of your grief. Some of these shifts will be temporary, but some will be profound, permanent changes in the way you think and act. Your sources of support in the grieving process may surprise you, but your sources of trouble and challenge as you go through these transitions may completely catch you off guard. Treat yourself as you would your best friend. With the help of people you trust, put safeguards in place to protect yourself from self-destructive behaviors or relationships where you could be exploited.

Chapter Fourteen

GUILT

*"She was no longer wrestling with her grief, but could sit down with it
as a lasting companion and make it a sharer in her thoughts."*

—George Eliot

G uilt is going to let go of you one slow inch at a time. Rationally,
I know I did nothing to cause my daughter's death. She was
with a trustworthy babysitter whom I knew well. This young
woman loved Virginia and took exemplary care of all the girls. They
were in a safe car going to a safe park on a beautiful Sunday afternoon.
What could have been more harmless? Yet even now, there are times
when I blame myself for Virginia's death, and the guilt is agonizing.

The worst of my guilt was behind me after about a year of counseling, but here I sit a decade later, and every few months, without warning,
those feelings of guilt bubble up again. In the early stages of my grief, I
berated myself every day. Why hadn't I insisted that the babysitter drive
my SUV to the park instead of her sedan? Why hadn't I kept Virginia in
a car seat a few months longer? What was I doing with a babysitter in the

first place? Did I really need that part-time job? Did my husband and I really need an occasional date night or a weekend away? Why wasn't I at home taking care of my children every minute of every day? I was brutal with myself.

I know that Dan experienced some of the same feelings. He said he felt guilty because he had left early on a Sunday afternoon for a work assignment that began on a Monday morning. He tortured himself thinking that if he had stayed home that Sunday afternoon, the girls might not have gone to the park in the first place.

Obviously, he hadn't done anything wrong at all. To the contrary, he was working hard to provide for his family. His guilt was as irrational as mine; he had been an exceptional parent. But just because guilt is usually irrational doesn't mean that it's not all-consuming and exhausting at times. As a mother, I felt my most important responsibility was to nurture and care for my daughters. I felt that I had failed and had paid the ultimate price as a consequence. I thought God was punishing me. Similarly, Dan felt that as a father, his most important job was to protect his daughters, yet despite his best efforts he was unable to shield them. Working through the guilt and learning how to cast off at least part of it is one of the toughest parts of the grief process.

The answer to resolving guilt is truly *time and process*, and an important factor in that process is accepting that while your guilt will get much lighter, it may never leave you completely. Another part of the process is discussing your grief in counseling over and over and over again. Each time you tell the story of how you could have or should have prevented your child's death, you'll hear more clearly how misguided and even arrogant those thoughts are. We are not in control, and once we accept that fact, we're better able to integrate our guilt into a more reasonable pattern of thinking. Even the most responsible parents cannot watch and protect their children every minute. To even attempt to do that would be to virtually imprison your children. They'd never ride in a car, never ride a bike, never learn to swim. To ski or get on a horse would be unthinkable.

Many of my friends have lost their children in drowning accidents, and I think their guilt may have been even more severe than mine. In every case, these children were close to their parents, and other adults were nearby when the accidents happened. These are diligent, responsible people who got distracted for a split second, and suddenly their children were gone.

As awful as drowning and automobile accidents are, the most horrific pain must be in the hearts of parents who have lost their sons or daughters to suicide or a drug overdose. Even though author David Scheff's son, Nick, survived his drug overdoses, the writer's gut-wrenching memoir about his son's methamphetamine addiction, *Beautiful Boy*, speaks to the horror of this with great clarity. The questions of "Why didn't I see this coming?" or "Why didn't I do something to prevent this?" must drive people to the edge of insanity. Yet, parents are often not the change agents in these situations. Almost without exception, every parent I know who has faced these ordeals has tried to do all they could for their children based on the information and resources they had at the time.

I used to get slightly impatient with these parents. After all, I reasoned, at least their child was *still alive*, and with that life came hope. My grief was worse—or was it? We can't calibrate a grief-and-guilt scale. We should never try to compare one parent's pain with another—it's all terrible. I have recently come to understand through personal experience and counseling that the grief parents bear when their children struggle with addiction, mental illness, or chronic disease can be nearly as painful as actually losing a child. It's beyond the scope of this book to explore all the differences and similarities in the guilt and constant anxiety faced in various situations, but I am challenged every day to show compassion to friends and family members who are living in the middle of that fire-storm. The finality of death is shattered for Christians by the promise of our faith, and I have had the opportunity to heal knowing that my child's spirit is with God and at peace. For parents whose children are struggling with addiction or mental illness, that terrible phone call or knock at the door is always lurking, and the specter of death or a fate worse than death for their child is constant. Being able to find any peace in that situation is nearly impossible. Reach out to these parents with extra kindness when you heal—we all know they could join our ranks any day.

In the end, the truth resonates: we are not in control. And of all the uncontrollable factors in the universe, what could be harder to rein in than the heart, mind, actions, and motivations of another human being? One of my favorite passages of Scripture is Romans 14:10–12, where Paul writes, "Why do you judge your brother? Or why do you show contempt for your brother? For we will all stand before the judgment seat of Christ . . . each of us will give an account of only himself to God." No matter how much we love our children or how well we think we know them, it is difficult, if not impossible, to fully fathom the intentions and actions of another person. Each of us has a secret heart known only to God.

Talk about your guilt. Pray. Pray hard and often. Forgive yourself, because God certainly forgives you. Odds are there was nothing to forgive in the first place.

Chapter Fifteen

THE BOOK OF JOB

"Everyone seeks answers, mostly to questions that are not very important. The great concern in life should be to discover which are the right questions. Then, even if you rarely get answers, you are at least journeying in the right direction."

—Paul Tillich

Of all the books I've read about grief since Virginia's death, none has been more important or more profound than the Old Testament book of Job. Strictly from a writer's perspective, Job is a beautiful piece of literature. Biblical scholars agree that Job was one of the earliest books written in the Bible, perhaps the very first. And while we'll never know with certainty who the author of Job was, I don't think anyone can argue with the insight of the writer, the poignancy of the subject matter, or the timing of when the book was written. As we've discussed before, the question of why innocent people suffer is one of the most perplexing in all of human experience.

Almost everyone knows the story of Job: God and Satan are chatting one afternoon after Satan shows up uninvited in the presence of the Creator. (I like to envision Satan crashing God's company picnic and softball game, and I see him sneaking around trying to filch beer out of the other angels' coolers.) Even in the formal language of older translations of the Bible, the conversation between God and the deceiver seems matter-of-fact, almost cordial. God asks Satan where he's been and what he's been doing lately, to which Satan replies, "I have been coming and going throughout the face of the Earth" (Job 1:7). You bet he has.

God responds by asking Satan if he's noticed a man in Uz named Job, who lives a blameless life and turns his back on temptation and evil. Satan answers by saying that sure, it's easy for a man like Job to be faithful and righteous—after all, he's got everything in the world going for him: land, cattle, a great family, and plenty of friends. But take any or all of that away, Satan quips, and Job would curse God immediately. Satan goes on to suggest that he'd be happy to test Job's faith to prove his point. Satan insists that Job loves his life and his possessions more than he loves God, and that at his core, Job is just as selfish and self-serving as any other man. God accepts Satan's challenge with one caveat: Satan can't kill Job.

The story unfolds, and Job eventually loses everything—and I do mean everything. At the end, Job is shivering in rags, he's covered from head to foot with painful ulcers, and all his children are dead. His wife is shouting hysterically that Job should curse God and die. To add to the torture, Job's three closest friends, Eliphaz, Bildad, and Zophar, come to visit Job and start handing out philosophical rhetoric about why Job is suffering in the first place and what he should do about it. What Job really needed from his friends was some ointment for his ulcers, a change of clothes, and a hot meal—certainly not all these judgments and platitudes.

The common expression "the patience of Job" would probably be more aptly called the "endurance of Job." Often Job is far from calm and stoic, but who can blame him? His suffering is unbearable. Job questions God, cries out to God for help, even rants and raves and screams at God. Like an incredibly patient father, God seems to be okay with all the complaining. The key to Job's story is that as miserable as Job becomes, he never turns his back on God and never completely abandons his faith. In the end, God and Satan acknowledge Job's faithfulness, and God starts to clean up his beleaguered follower. Job's fortunes are restored, the ulcers heal, and he gets brand-new cattle and kids. Happy ending, right? Wrong. Cattle and tents might be replaceable and interchangeable, but children certainly aren't. Job's grief over the death of his children can't be wiped away even by the joy of new babies. Certainly these new children will help Job heal, but they aren't substitutes, and they can't make up for what has been lost.

Once you've lost a child, you read the book of Job with fresh eyes. I had read Job before Virginia was killed, but when I looked at the Scripture again several months after the accident, answers about why and how bad things happen to the innocent suddenly seemed clearer. Obviously God and Satan aren't literally striking deals to torture and test people; the message of Job is in the allegory of suffering and our reaction to it. I came to the conclusion that if we can somehow hang on to some shred of our faith even as we grieve and suffer, then God will restore us partially in this life and fully in the life to come.

In the final chapters of Job, God draws close to Job and tells him (and thereby all of us) that Job can't possibly comprehend the complexities of the universe or why things happen the way they do. God is the only one who understands the "laws of the heavens" (Job 38:33), and he is the only one with the wisdom to give the cues in nature as to when deer fawn and trees bud. He's in charge, and trying to explain the workings of the cosmos to humanity is simply impossible. We don't have the intellectual or spiritual hardware to run the programs. And for those of us who choose to read even more closely, I think God is also hinting that managing this expanding universe, with millions of galaxies and mysterious dark matter, isn't always easy even for him. The last verses of Job describe the Leviathan, an unspeakable monster that has to be contained. In literal terms, leviathans were probably the huge crocodiles that menaced people and livestock from the rivers and marshes of biblical times. They were man-eaters. But the Leviathan of Job is more than a nasty reptile at the top of the food chain. The Leviathan of Job is a powerful symbol, an allegory for our physical universe and all the suffering and chaos that exists within it.

Over and over again, not only in Job but also throughout the Old and New Testaments, God seems to be saying, "You've got to trust me on this one. You can't fully understand what is happening or why, even though the struggle to make sense of your world is a fundamental part of the human experience. Stick with me, hang on tight through this wild, sometimes nightmarish ride of life, and I'll see you through to the other side. I'll never abandon you, and when we get off this roller coaster, I'll be able to explain the purpose of all this pain and joy in a language you can understand."

I'll bet I read Job half a dozen times in the year after Virginia died, and every time I closed my Bible when I finished, I felt a sense of peace. I wouldn't recommend trying to read Job during the initial days of your grief, though. Give yourself some time, maybe a couple of months, and then look at the Scripture. When you do feel strong enough to read Job, I hope that you, too, will feel solace and healing from the message.[12]

Chapter Sixteen

THE LEGACY OF YOUR CHILD'S LIFE

"If you were all alone in the universe with no one to talk to,
no one with whom to share the beauty of the stars, to laugh with,
to touch, what would be your purpose in life? It is other life,
it is love which gives your life meaning."

—Mitsugi Saotome

Earlier I wrote some biting remarks about the top ten awful things people said to friends of mine and to me after the death of our children. Now I want to tell you about the most comforting things people said to me after Virginia died. Without a doubt, the most beautiful message came to me from a woman I'll call Claire, who came to see my family at the visitation the night before Virginia's funeral. She hugged me and said, "Every life, no matter how short or long, has great purpose and worth. It may take a little time for you all to fully understand how important Virginia's life was, but one day you will."

I was stunned. After Claire made that statement, I felt like someone had taken a light and placed it at the end of a dark tunnel. I immediately felt comfort; my pain faded for a moment. I knew Claire was right. She'd held up a beacon of hope for me.

What did your child's life teach you? What did it teach the people around you, and how did your child's life, or even the circumstances of illness or death, make the world a better place? Even in the worst days of your grief you'll get flashes of the answer, and when you are able to embrace the concept that your child's life, no matter how brief or painful, has been meaningful, then letting go and healing become easier. At least, that was the case for me.

Long after Virginia's death, I met the extraordinary man who would eventually become my best friend, my other half, and years later, my husband. I was training for the Marine Corps Marathon in Washington DC. He was a mentor and running coach for the Leukemia and Lymphoma Society's Team in Training program, and from the fund-raising and informational letter that every volunteer runner sends out, he knew that I was running not only in tribute to the little girl from Atlanta who was our Honored Hero and a leukemia survivor, but also in honor and in memory of Virginia. We met for coffee one morning before he had to go to the funeral of a close friend's teenage daughter. He had known this girl since she was a young child, and he was distraught over her death. He wanted to know what in the world he could do or say to offer some meaningful comfort to his friend and their family. He also asked me where I was in my grieving process. That was the first time I clearly remember articulating the legacy of Virginia's life and its full impact on me.

"She taught me," I said, "never to miss a chance to tell the people you love how much you care about them. She taught me never to waste a day in settling arguments or setting things right with friends or family. We never know how much time we've got with each other. Every day, every breath, is a gift from God. She taught me joy, and she taught me that today is all we have. We can't take anyone or anything for granted." Once I said those things out loud, I knew that I had cleared another hurdle in the grieving process. Virginia's lessons had outlived her.

Virginia was a gorgeous, ethereal little sprite who was always dancing, incessantly talking, and constantly dazzling everyone around her with her brilliant blue eyes and her unforgettable cross-bite smile. She was not, however, a saint. Not for a second. She was mischievous, she was vain, and her sisters and I often joked that we would have had to watch her like a hawk once she got to middle school, because even at age five she was a notorious flirt. She used to taunt her older sisters by saying, "Daddy loves me the best because I'm the prettiest." Needless to say, statements like that did not endear her to her siblings!

Recognizing and admitting your child's foibles as well as gifts is another clear sign that you're healing. In the early stages of grief, it's easy to venerate the child you've lost. It's normal, it's natural. Don't beat yourself up as you do it, and as much as possible, allow your spouse and especially the grandparents the same latitude. In time, though, you'll come to grieve the real person, the total person, with all the good and bad traits. That sense of loss will be much deeper and more painful, but in the end the pain will be more authentic and allow you to heal more completely.

My mother died a little over a year before Virginia's accident, and in the time when my mom's health was declining, I took the girls as often as I could to visit my parents in the small town near Savannah, Georgia, where I grew up. My mother had two wonderful friends there—smart, capable women with great hearts and great wits. They had nicknamed my mother "Magnolia" because of her heavy Southern drawl and her obsession with clothes. My mother easily owned a hundred pairs of shoes and even more handbags.

My mother's friends immediately dubbed Virginia "Little Magnolia" as they watched her ransack my mother's closets and jewelry boxes in search of fashion-accessory treasures. There was no denying Virginia's genes; she was her grandmother all over again. Mom's friends also howled as I told them about Virginia petting a lady's sable coat in church one Sunday and asking where she might get one too. Our favorite story, however, was about a question Virginia asked a lady in our congregation who had some beautiful pieces of antique jewelry that she wore one morning to a church breakfast. "Miss Joy," Virginia asked, "can I have your jewelry when you get old or when you die?" I thought I would die at the moment Virginia asked that.

Joy didn't crack a smile, but she winked at me and said, "Virginia, if you want this jewelry one day, I'm afraid you'll have to marry my son."

Virginia looked Joy straight in the eye and said, "Okay, where is he?"

Are you getting a snapshot of this child's hilarious personality and a glimpse of the woman she would have become one day? Funny and endearing, utterly charming, but not without some spice. Another part of Virginia's legacy was to teach me to love and accept both the good and the less-than-ideal traits in others, because often it's the quirks in character that make people most loveable and certainly the most interesting!

Several months after Virginia died, one of my mother's friends called me and told me she'd had a dream about my mom. She said, "I don't mean to upset you, but I had the most vivid dream last night about Marion and Virginia. I dreamed your mom was standing with open arms to catch and hug Virginia as Ginny was running toward her." Upset me? Far, far from it. That image of my mother reaching out to embrace her granddaughter is one of the most comforting thoughts I will ever have.

As you move forward through your grief, your memories of your child will become more varied and complex. You'll remember times of laughter and great tenderness with your child, but you'll also remember occasions when you were impatient or even angry. You'll be taking a fuller, more authentic view of a real human being, not an idealized image. Admitting all that you've lost in your child, good and bad, will ultimately bring you to greater healing.

Chapter Seventeen

MEMORY AND RECOLLECTION

"It's not so much that we're afraid of change or so in love with the old ways—it's that place in between that we fear. It's like flying between trapezes. It's Linus when his blanket is in the dryer. There is nothing to hold on to."

—Marilyn Ferguson

The day will come when you will need to go through your child's clothes, toys, and school records. You will need to pack up most of these things and put them away. I don't need to tell you how tough that day will be. I know of a couple whose friends came into their home and stored all of the child's belongings before the family even got back from the funeral. I'm sure those friends had only the best intentions, but I thought it was a terribly misguided action. Sorting through your child's things is one of the most intensely personal experiences of life, and it will be an unforgettable milestone in the grieving process for you and your spouse. Only you can determine when the time is right; you are not on anyone else's timetable. And this is one of those rare instances in life where you really *are* in control.

You may want to pack everything alone as I did, or you and your spouse may elect to go through your child's possessions together. Be sensitive to each other's needs: if one person isn't ready, then wait; but conversely, if months and months have gone by and you haven't been able to face the ordeal of putting things away, respect your partner's need to move on and clear this hurdle. You may choose to put away your child's belongings with the help of friends, or you may want to have someone else do it for you. Do what feels most comfortable for you; everyone's needs and feelings are different. I put away or gave away nearly everything Virginia had, but I kept a few of her prized possessions out of sight but close at hand: her favorite books and a mangled, ragged teddy bear that Virginia named Zsa Zsa. (I have Zsa Zsa II; Ginny is buried with Zsa Zsa I. Every canny mom knows that if you can find duplicates of favorite stuffed animals, grab them. If one is lost or gets so filthy that the Health Department is lurking at your door, you've got backup!) I also kept dozens of pieces of her artwork from the Day School, and of course, I have that pencil-box collection of rocks and twigs. I keep all these items in a cedar chest along with Virginia's christening gown and some special pieces of clothing. I have albums full of photographs of Virginia, and Daniel has hours of videotape of Virginia's conversations and parties.

At some level, many people feel that if they begin to heal, then they will begin to forget their lost child. I can assure you that won't happen. You will never forget your child, but the focus will blur, the memory will soften, and in a few years you will come to the point where you have a handful of days when you don't actively think about the child you've lost. That's okay; that's normal too. You, as the parent, will always carry the deepest and most active memory of the child. Siblings, grandparents, and close friends will remember too, but not the way you will. You can't expect them to; life moves on for everyone. A few of my best friends still remember Virginia's birthday or the anniversary of the accident, and it touches and affirms me every time they mention her name or the date.

I can still remember Virginia's voice, but it is fading. That fading voice makes the videotapes we have of Virginia even more precious. I'm not now in a position where I feel comfortable asking my ex-husband for copies of the tapes, but perhaps one day I will, and for now, simply knowing that the tapes exist is enough. For several years, I didn't wipe Virginia's handprints from the windowpanes, and I didn't try to scrub away the crayon marks she had left on one of the walls in her bedroom. One day, on your own timetable and on your own terms, you'll be ready to clean the windows and the wall, but there is no need to rush.

Write down the best memories you have of your child, and encourage your close friends and family to do the same. A scrapbook or a journal of your child's life can be one of the most comforting possessions you'll ever have, especially in the later stages of your grief. Several members of our church prepared a scrapbook of Virginia's artwork and some photos from Vacation Bible School and Sunday school classes over the years, and they included some of their own memories of Virginia or their own children's memories of her. They gave that incredible gift to our family about a year after the accident. Words can't describe how touched we were by that gesture. As you heal, you may want to frame a piece of your child's artwork or a photograph of him or her. Over time (and plenty of it), you will find that the symbols and tangible objects from your child's life will become reminders of joy, not of loss and pain.

Some people visit their child's grave site frequently, some not at all. This too is an intensely personal choice. One of the most powerful moments in my healing came during the summer after Virginia's death.

Debbie Schecter suggested that we go by the cemetery to visit her son's grave site and Virginia's. It was a blistering hot August afternoon, and we stopped at the florist counter of the grocery store to pick up bouquets of flowers before we drove to the cemetery. As we drove past the cemetery gates, Debbie headed over to Virginia's grave site first, not her son's, and she motioned for me to get out of the car.

"Betsy," she said, "right now this is a painful, tough place for you, I know. This is where you have to come to feel physically close to your child, but you also know Virginia is not here; her spirit is not here. Give it time, and you'll feel her less and less in this place, but more and more in your heart, and in the places where she lived and played. This place, this cemetery, will become less important.

"Hold on to the family you've got left," she continued, "and try to hold on to your faith, and you'll heal. Jews don't typically bring flowers to grave sites, Bets. All these flowers are for Virginia and for you."

I cannot imagine anyone being a more compassionate friend than Debbie Schecter was to me that day. We stood at Virginia's grave site and cried for a minute or two, and then we drove over to her son's headstone where we placed a few smooth pebbles, and we cried some more. Debbie was right. Neither one of our children is in that place; our children's spirits, the real part of them, are with God. The cemetery and the grave sites are nothing more than places to go where we place flowers or pebbles. They are serene parks where we can be quiet with our memories for a little while. Go as often as you need to your child's grave, stay as long as you must, but don't stay too long. Your life is waiting for you, your child's legacy is waiting for you, and your child would be impatient for you to leave this place of sadness and get busy living again.

My neighbor told me that after her father and brother were killed in an automobile accident, her mother simply closed the door to her brother's bedroom. Nothing was ever touched; nothing was ever changed. I will never stand in judgment about how anyone chooses to deal with death and loss, but for my friend, her brother's room became a forbidden and sealed place—a place she could only associate with death. The closed door became a symbol of loss and hopelessness, not of her brother's life, and it faced her every time she walked down the hall as she was growing up.

Do what you must. Honor and remember your child in whatever way works for you. I worked with a dozen people in our congregation to construct a nature walk on the church grounds in memory of Virginia and several other members' children who had died, and a Sunday-school room was refurbished and equipped with interactive educational materials through memorial donations and the amazing vision of two women on our session. Ron Greer and his wife built a playground in honor of their son, and another friend's family dedicated a park in tribute to their little boy. The families of the Day School made contributions which paid for a Victorian-style playhouse on the school grounds, and while the children who play there now have no idea who Virginia was, the pure fun they have in that playhouse is one of the best legacies I can imagine for her life.

Don't feel obligated to do anything public or elaborate to commemorate your child's life. For the first year or two of your grief, and perhaps even longer, you may not have the energy or financial resources to do anything at all. Your memorials may all be private, contained within your own prayers and thoughts or expressed in simple words or acts of kindness to other people. That too is a beautiful tribute, and it is more than enough.

Chapter Eighteen

A SHOULDER TO LEAN ON

*"When we honestly ask ourselves which persons in our lives mean
the most to us, we often find that it is those who, instead of giving much
advice, solutions, or cures, have chosen rather to share our pain
and touch our wounds with a gentle and tender hand.
The friend who can be silent with us in a moment of despair or confusion,
who can stay with us in an hour of grief and bereavement,
who can tolerate not knowing, not curing, not healing, and face with us
the reality of our powerlessness, that is a friend who cares."*

—Henri Nouwen

E ven as bereaved parents, we often wonder what to say or do to best
offer compassion to others who have lost children. What is most
comforting and meaningful to friends and family members who
are grieving? Conversely, what should we *avoid* saying or doing to make
an unspeakable situation even worse? I've talked to dozens of bereaved
parents in researching this chapter, and while every culture and faith has
different mores and expectations about grief and sympathy, I can tell

you that with very few exceptions, if you'll follow the suggestions listed
below, you'll provide the solace and the practical help that your friends
or family members need most.

1. All you really need to say to bereaved parents, especially
   in the first hours and days after their child's death, is
   that you are deeply sorry for their loss and that you are
   constantly thinking about them. That expression means
   even more when it's paired with a hug.

2. Send a letter or card, not just an e-mail, to the family that has lost the child. Follow up that card or letter
   with another, or with a phone call a few weeks later.
   Many families receive an outpouring of support in the
   initial days after the child's death, but most of that support fades quickly. The bereaved family will need your
   attention even more as the grief process moves forward.

3. Take a meal to the family. A platter of sandwiches for
   lunch or a tray of fresh fruit is every bit as welcome as a
   full dinner.

4. Take a walk with your friend or with the entire family.
   Don't feel compelled to talk too much, if at all. Let your
   friend have the luxury of quiet and the gift of someone
   who will truly listen. Remember the lessons from Job
   and his verbose, self-righteous buddies. Sometimes the
   more you say, the more painful it gets.

5. If you say you're going to pray for someone, be sure to
   do it. Nothing is as empty or cold as the promise of a
   prayer that you doubt will ever be given.

6. Bring your friend a book about dealing with grief and
   loss, but be sure you've read it first. You'll have a good

idea from the tone of the book whether your friends will be ready to process the basic themes the writer is trying to convey. Books that deal with controversial issues of religion and the afterlife may be better saved for later.

7. Plant a tree in the child's memory, and do everything you can to make sure the tree survives. A tree that grows and prospers in a place where the grieving family can see it is one of the most healing, powerful symbols of hope and the regeneration of life.

8. Dedicate a race. If you're a runner, biker, or walker, participate in a local road race, and let the family know that your effort and any money you might raise for charity will be done in their child's memory. Similarly, any donation you make to a charity directly or to sponsor someone else in a race is an incredibly supportive gesture. My running partners ran the Savannah-Tybee half marathon with me a couple of years after Virginia died, and two of our non-running friends met us at the finish line with buttons that carried Virginia's picture. It was touching, and it was also great fun and a step back into normalcy for me.

9. Prepare a meal for a charity or for its volunteers. Swing a hammer for a Habitat house, or sort clothes for a homeless shelter. Donations don't have to be monetary. You'll recall that my older daughters' Girl Scout troop and their moms prepared dinner for the families and staff at the Ronald McDonald House in Virginia's memory, and the interaction and service to others was a perfect way to honor her.

10. Use the child's name in conversation. Many people are afraid they'll upset their friends by bringing up the child's name and the memory of the child's death. You won't. Believe me, your friends are thinking constantly about their child already. You aren't bringing up something painful that has dropped out of their conscious thought. The real fear bereaved parents have is that their child will be forgotten. When you say their child's name, you let them know that you are still thinking about their child too.

11. Respect your friends' need for privacy, but if you are a close friend, be watchful for signs of alcohol or drug abuse as the grief process continues. Be discreet and compassionate, but keep your friends alert about relationships and behaviors that could be destructive to them or their family in the long run.

12. In matters of faith, keep your opinions about God's will and your thoughts about heaven, hell, and the afterlife to yourself for a little while. If your friends want to talk about these issues, by all means listen, but do your best to keep quiet about spiritual matters, especially if you disagree with your friends' beliefs. The time will come when you can discuss these questions, but the first year or two after a child's death can be a period of spiritual turmoil and doubt for these parents. This is a time for gentle support, not debate or proselytizing.

13. Walk the dog, do the laundry, mow the lawn. Grieving parents are usually exhausted physically as well as emotionally. The act of folding a load of laundry or running

the vacuum cleaner speaks volumes about your love and concern for a bereaved family.

14. Remember the surviving children. Siblings are grieving too, and something as simple as bringing them books or craft supplies or taking them out for pizza is healing for them and the entire family.

15. Don't gossip about the family or the circumstances of the child's death, and don't allow others to gossip or speculate either. Gossip, that most subtle and insidious brand of evil, often begins as earnest conversation and concern about a family. You'll know, though, when discussion crosses the line. Refuse to participate in gossip. One woman told me how the details of Virginia's accident and her injuries had been discussed over and over again in a carpool line, and I was too upset to even respond.

16. Bring a photograph or put together a scrapbook with a group of people. If you have a candid photograph of the child who has died, you may want to consider framing that photograph and giving it to the family a few weeks or months after the child's funeral. The gesture may be too emotional for the family in the earliest stages of grief, but later, having a framed photograph will be especially meaningful. Do not, under any circumstances, send digital photographs via e-mail or especially Facebook. That forum is too public and impersonal.

17. Don't try to compare the loss of a spouse, parent, or sibling with the loss of a child. All of those losses are terrible and heartbreaking, but the relationships are too

different for comparison, and trying to tell a grieving parent that you understand their loss because you've lost an older family member may actually be hurtful to your bereaved friend.

Chapter Nineteen

INTO THE LIGHT

"Move forward into the Light."
—Barbara Kingsolver, *The Poisonwood Bible*

M ost bereaved parents say, as they resolve their grief and heal, that all they want is peace. It's true. We aren't looking for the sort of happiness we had in our lives before we lost our children, because we'll forever live with a sense of loss. Our priorities have changed, and in many ways, both good and bad, we are fundamentally different people than we were before we lost a son or daughter. We may find joy and love in our lives again, and hopefully we'll also find a renewed sense of purpose in our family, work, and community, but our perspectives about all of our relationships are forever altered.

My friend, a journalist, has the uncanny ability to get enormous disclosure from people with a simply worded, direct question. She asked me not too long ago, "Betsy, do you think Virginia's death redeemed you?" On the surface, that might have seemed an odd, even offensive question, but I've known this woman a long time, and I knew the intent of what she was asking. The answer was clearly yes on several levels.

I know now, as you do, that we can't take people or the time we have with them for granted; we know each minute is a gift. You and I also realize that lightning can strike twice. The fact that we've lost one child doesn't protect us in any way from losing another child or a grandchild. And as time becomes such a treasured commodity, we can't afford to waste any of it on relationships or individuals who are not genuine. Our new circumstances force us to change our lives and live authentically. Worn-out social traditions and mores don't work for us anymore; we have to redefine who we are and what we want out of life. It's a painful transition, but to do otherwise would be to betray the legacy of our children's lives.

Our faith and our relationship with God are forever altered too. The unanswerable questions of why tragedy must claim innocent children will keep us beating our heads against the wall until the day we die, I suppose. I don't think God minds if we are constantly grappling for those answers. He simply wants us to hold on to the strands of faith and trust him for the answers in the life to come. We have to be patient. We have to wait for the answers we need. Einstein said in the closing years of his life, "God does not play dice with the universe." Maybe not, but the universe at times seems to be playing dice with us. Often it appears as though random chance is the only force at work in determining why some people live while others die. Only God has the answers.

I hope you find love, support, and compassion from everyone around you as you work through your grief. I hope you find an able counselor, and I hope you find a friend with a heart as big as Montana with whom you can cry and share your top-ten-awful-things list at the end of a long walk. I hope you can hold your marriage together and find renewed love and intimacy. I pray you are forever healing and that time will reveal the full purpose of your child's life. I pray you will have the courage, the health, and the resources to fulfill the legacy of your child's life, and more than anything, I pray that you will always feel the overwhelming comfort of Christ's presence as you grieve. He is always there. Always. We were not meant to face this pain alone. We have in Christ a constant guide and light in the darkness. I hope you find peace.

"And lo, I am with you always, even unto the end of the age" (Matthew 28:20).

1 Kubler-Ross, Elizabeth, *On Death and Dying,* New York, NY: Macmillan: 1969.

2 Kubler-Ross, Elizabeth, *On Children and Death,* New York, NY: Simon & Schuster: 1983. 43–50; 167–170.

3 Maciejewski, Paul K., PhD; Zhang, Baohui, MS, et al. "An Empirical Examination of the Stage Theory of Grief," JAMA, Vol. 297, No. 7, February 21, 2007.

4 Ibid.

5 Sanders, Catherine M., PhD, *How to Survive the Loss of a Child,* Three Rivers Press, 1992. 20–22.

6 Rando, Teresa, "Bereaved Parents: Particular Difficulties, Unique Factors, and Treatment Issues," *Social Work,* Vol. 30, 1985; 20.

7 Striof, Sherry and Robert, "The Unthinkable Grief—the Death of a Child and the Impact of Grief on Marriage," About. com:Marriage. June 2008.

8   Murphy, Shirley, PhD., et al. "Challenging the Myths About
     Parents' Adjustment After the Sudden, Violent Death of a Child,"
     Journal of Nursing Scholarship, Vol. 35, No. 4. April 23, 2004.
     359–364.

9   Lazar, S.W., G. Bush, R.L. Gollub, et al. "Functional Brain
     Mapping of the Relaxation Response and Meditation,"
     NeuroReport, 2000, Vol. 11. 1581–1585.
     Lou, H.C., T.W. Kjaier, L. Friberg, et al. "A150-h20 PET Study
     of Meditation and the Resting State of Normal Consciousness,"
     Human Brain Mapping, 1999, Vol. 7. 98–105.
     Newberg, A.B., A. Alavi, M. Baime, et al. "The Measurement of
     Regional Cerebral Blood Flow During the Complex Cognitive
     Task of Meditation: a Preliminary SPECT Study," *Psychiatry
     Research: Neuroimaging,* 2002, Vol. 106. 113–122.
     Newburg, A.B., M. Pourdehnad, A. Alavi, E. d'Aquilli. "Cerebral
     Blood Flow during Meditative Prayer: Preliminary Findings and
     Methodological Issues," *Perceptual and Motor Skills,* 2003, Vol. 97.
     630–635.

10   Preston, John D., Psy.D. *Integrative Treatment for Borderline
     Personality Disorder,* New Harbinger Publications, Oakland,
     California, 2006. 18–23.

11   Personal interview with Elizabeth Donnelly, M.S. educational
     consultant. January 18, 2010.

12   Since I wrote the initial draft of chapter 15, I've had the good
     fortune to be able to take a class in Biblical Canon from the
     Chairman of Old Testament Studies at Columbia Seminary. From

that class I learned that in the earliest written versions of Job, the concept of monotheism appears to be just taking root, and Satan and the angels are sometimes referred to as "gods"—small 'g'—or minor deities. The meeting in the first chapter of Job seems to describe a type of council meeting between God and the angels. Also, biblical scholars and archaeologists now agree that passages in the book of Exodus are actually the oldest written passages in the Bible, with the book of Job coming after them. The Leviathan, the monster described in the last chapters of Job, is sometimes thought to be a crocodile, sometimes a whale. The particular type of animal doesn't seem as important as the allegorical power and danger that the beast conveys.